Christian Youth Work

Christian Youth Work

Mark Ashton and Phil Moon
Updated by Jonathan Carswell

10 Publishing
a division of 10ofthose.com

First published by Kingsway Publications 1986
Revised edition 1995

Second edition published in 2007 by Authentic Media

Published in 2010 by 10Publishing, a division of 10ofthose.com
Unit 19 Common Bank Industrial Estate
Ackhurst Road
Chorley
PR7 1NH
Email: info@10ofthose.com
Website: www.10ofthose.com

British Library Cataloguing in Publication Data

A catalogue record for this book is available from the British Library

ISBN 978-1-90617-320-3

The authors of Christian Youth Work are no longer able to document some of the quotations in this book. If they are ever able to locate this information they will include it in any subsequent editions.

Cover Design by David McNeill
Print Management by Printbridge

For Fiona and Anna

Contents

Acknowledgements

The original version of this book was published in 1986 and written by Mark alone, who acknowledged at that point almost every friend he had in youth work (in the hope they might buy a copy). It would not be appropriate to list those names again now (although Mark still wants to acknowledge his debt to them).

Mark and Phil were both employed by the Church Pastoral Aid Society, in the work of CYFA (the Church Youth Fellowships Association), working with church-based youth groups in the Anglican Church. The generous support and encouragement of our colleagues in the Youth and Children's Division of CPAS (CYPECS) allowed us to write the book in the first place, so we owe a large debt of gratitude to them, and to all the countless churches throughout the UK who by their giving to CPAS made the work of CYFA possible.

Introduction

In 1981 Mark Ashton started work with CYFA, to help the work of the local church with older teenagers. One glance told him that this was an area of frightening weakness. In so many churches the older teenagers were the scarcest members of the congregation. He could see a few encouraging signs of life, but the overwhelming impression was that Christians had not thought out their approach to teenagers.

Over two decades later, we are not doing much better. At best, we are perhaps now just more aware of our weaknesses in this area. We see and hear that teenagers are flooding out of the church, and many are familiar with the by now infamous statistic that 'over 1,000 young people are leaving the church each week'.

Why is this happening?

Some youth workers major on finding sociological answers, and therefore seek to understand and relate to youth culture. Others search for psychological solutions, and take as their starting point an examination of what makes young people tick. Others seek ecclesiastical solutions, and argue for a revolution in our churches in order to keep hold of the young people we do have and to bring in more teenagers.

All these approaches have much to teach us about young people, and we need to learn from them if we are to have an effective youth ministry. But these cannot be our starting point.

Christians have subconsciously assumed that the Bible has little to teach us about young people growing up in the twenty-first century. The weakness of Christian youth work today is a result. Christian youth work must be different from all other forms of youth work. It must be distinct in its aim, because Christians have a unique view of what it is to be a human being. And Christian youth work must be distinct in its methods, because God has provided us with guidelines for understanding adolescence in our own particular culture, and has not left us at the mercy of contemporary fashions in the social sciences.

This book is not a systematic theology of youth, written by academic theologians. Neither is it a practical handbook of church youth work. But it is concerned with theory and it is concerned with theology. It is written out of a great desire to give Christians a renewed vision for young people, a new confidence in what they can do for them, how they can do it, and why they should do it. But our theory and our theology should affect our practice, and so at the end of each chapter there is a response section which suggests how to think through the content of the chapter in order to put it into practice. Some of the ideas are for the individual, some can be worked through by a team of leaders.

We have tried not to tell the stories of our friends. There have been a number of good books telling stories of youth work. The approach here is theoretical rather than anecdotal. Obviously, we refer in passing to our own experiences with young people, but we do not think that what we have done should, in itself, be accorded any authority. The most important test is not that the ideas in this book work in practice (which they do), but that they come from, and are true to, the Bible. This book follows one practice which you may find irritating. When writing about youth leaders and young people, we have deliberately switched genders regularly. It seems a good way of avoiding giving the impression that youth ministry is reserved for one sex or the other. It may be disconcerting, but it makes an important point.

The years from thirteen to twenty do not have a special value above that of other ages, but they are significant for the personal development of the individual. In young people we see a microcosm of society and, very often, a thermometer of the health of the nation and the church. Much of what follows applies to adults as well as to teenagers, because the spiritual principles are the same – but their application varies depending on the age of the people we are working with. It is not the task of this book to make that application, but we are well aware how wide the discussion could become at some points.

This is not a book for young people. It is a book for adults concerned about young people and the church. The church is the body of Christ. Whether we like the idea or not, the church (in all its forms and failures) is where Jesus is in the world today. He has a heart for the young. So must we, if we would be faithful to him, and if we would fulfil his commission to the young people of our day.

Foreword

We are told that when major events occur we can remember exactly where we were at the time. Reading Mark Ashton's *Christian Youth Work* was a major event in my ministry amongst young people and I vividly remember how I first came across it. It received a rave review in a journal and so I bought my own copy (which, much thumbed, I still retain) and was not disappointed.

At that stage I had already been involved in youth work for about fifteen years and in all that time had not read anything remotely like this. Here was a book which had a genuinely biblical approach to youth work. It did not pay lip service to the Bible's role in youth ministry but saw it as essential to all that was done amongst adolescents. Whilst it showed a keen awareness of youth culture it did not allow this to hijack the goals and conduct of week-in week-out work with churched teens. Whilst it saw evangelism as a key part of any programme it also saw that this was best achieved through discipleship, as Jesus himself commanded in Matthew 28:19, 20. Whilst it showed an understanding of adolescence it rightly identified teenagers as those best equipped to witness to most of their peers and see them saved. The implications, not only for youth work, but for the role of the youth worker were significant.

This new edition brings those same strengths to all of us who have an involvement with and concern for the rising generation in and outside our churches. If you serve in youth work in any way, if you are a minister or a parent, then this book is essential reading. It will enable you to chart the waters of youth ministry as well as giving you insight into what is needed to build disciples for the church of Jesus Christ.

It may be surprising that a book about youth work, which first saw the light of day in 1986 and was revised by Mark Ashton and Phil Moon in 1996, should now be republished some twenty years later. Haven't times moved on? Aren't today's adolescents markedly different to they were ten let alone twenty years ago? Of course, but their essential need to enjoy life under the loving rule of the God who made them remains the same. This is why the message of this book remains timeless.

It has long been a source of regret to me that *Christian Youth Work* was no longer in print and I am therefore delighted that it is being made available once more. It is also an enormous source of relief that I shall no longer have to tell my students to scour the internet to find a second-hand copy of this excellent book.

Ian Fry
Director of Youth and Children's Ministry Training,
Oak Hill College
September 2006

1. Gray's Anatomy, Michelin Guide or Instruction Book?

The biblical basis for youth work

Youth decay

The bishop listened intently to the church's steel band. Clearly, the racial mix of teenagers playing their animated West Indian rhythms had captured his interest.

'Do they come to church at all?' he asked.

'Oh yes, and we have a Bible study meeting each week as well,' the youth leader replied.

'You mean these young people actually read the Bible?' The episcopal eyebrows were raised in astonishment.

The Christian church is not doing well with teenagers. There is quite a bit of work with children, but after thirteen, most local churches of whatever denomination (or none) find it hard going. 'Youth decay' is now setting in earlier than ever before. We used to be able to keep them until they were fourteen. Now, if they make it to fourteen we reckon we've done well, and we've then got a reasonable chance of keeping them through their teenage years.

These feelings are supported by Peter Brierley's statistics. Previously, it was clear that many teenagers are leaving the church: '13 per cent of English teenagers attended church in 1979, only 9 per cent were doing so in 1989. In 1979, 960,000 young people aged 10–19 attended church. In 1989, this age band of young people were 10 years older, and in the 20–29 age band only 490,000 attended church, a forty-nine per cent drop in church attendance.'[1] In the last decade this problem has intensified. Despite a population increase the attendance of young people at UK churches has continued to drop. And there appears to be no arrest in the decline. The projected figures for the coming years predict that by 2016 the number of those under fifteen attending church will be as low as 225,000.[2]

Youth decay sets in. For every church fellowship that has a flourishing group of teenagers in its membership, there are three with no children's or youth work at all.[3]

So is the whole teenage subculture becoming a no-go area for the Christian faith?

There has been no shortage of thought and energy expended in the attempt to reach young people with the gospel. Youth culture has been analysed and infiltrated by Christians. Pete Ward, formerly of Oxford Youth Works, wrote: 'As a Christian youthworker I live in two worlds. The first world is created by young people themselves. This is the continually changing bright and alive world of youth culture . . . The other world that I live in is similar; it's the world of the Gospel.'[4]

Much has been written about youth culture, and some of us reckon we are beginning to understand it. In the world of music, arts festivals, road shows, magazines, sport and the media, excellent work has been done. We know how to relate to teenagers. We know what they like and what they don't like. We know how to amuse them. And sometimes we think we know how to reach out to them.

For over four decades the attention of the churches has been drawn to the disadvantaged young people of the inner cities. Open youth projects, outreach programmes, skills centres and community work have been organised and run by Christians. Christian pressure groups have been set up, aiming to change the structures of society in order to help those young people who are alienated from the world in which they live. The plight of rural young people, with their special problems of isolation and limited resources, has not escaped attention either. And the drive to work with the under-privileged continues. Youth for Christ (YFC), in its strategy for the nineties, stated:

> YFC will move out from a primarily youth ministry role amongst those currently reached by the church, to working amongst the vast majority of young people who are outside the church. YFC will move from *the grasslands of youth ministry to the dark jungle of youth culture.* This will mean a bias to the poor, the needy and to the under-privileged in society.[5]

So why, with all this effort and activity, does the outlook remain so bleak? Are the churches being bypassed by the Spirit of God? Is he now at work in ways and in places that we find hard to perceive? Or do we need to redefine the gospel in order to make it more relevant to young people in the twenty-first century?

Or is it just that the Christian faith is actually on an irretrievable decline in the western world – a decline most apparent among young people? Has the sea of faith finally ebbed away, and must we now find new ways of defining and speaking about God? Or has our Christian thinking been so infiltrated by secularism, materialism and post-modern thinking that we are blind to the will of God for his people and to his plans to establish his kingdom?

The challenge

Perhaps some of the answers to the Christian faith's decaying impact on teenagers may lie closer at hand than we think. The existence of a youth-orientated popular culture is so recent, so brash and so dominant, that it is easy to see it as an entirely new phenomenon, posing questions that have never been asked before. It is tempting to believe that the youth decay of the church springs from a failure to understand this new culture, rather than a failure to understand the faith.

But the most serious weakness in Christian ministry among teenagers today is not a failure to understand our culture. It is a failure to take the Bible sufficiently seriously.

There are two fundamental necessities in Christian communication. One is that we take the world we live in seriously; and the other is that we take God's revelation to us in the Bible seriously. If either is missing, the communication will be ineffective.

However, either of these necessities may become all-absorbing. We can strive so hard to be relevant to young people that we immerse ourselves in their culture to a point where the distinctiveness of the Christian message vanishes. Or we can be so concerned to be faithful to the Bible that we forget that the culture of the Bible and the culture of our world are miles apart. We then drive an unbiblical wedge between evangelism and social action; or we throw up our hands in horror at the thought of using rock music as a medium to communicate the gospel – the 'They didn't have it then, so we can't possibly use it now' syndrome.

However, if we have to err on one side or the other, we must not lose our hold on Christian truth. The simple message of God's love for sinful humanity and of his forgiveness of our sins for the sake of his son has extraordinary and immense power: our incompetence as communicators is not able to destroy its ability to reach non-Christian young people.

That is why some Christian youth work is characterised by two apparently irreconcilable extremes. On the one hand, it is massively irrelevant to any young person. Yet, on the other hand, it does, undeniably, change human lives.

There is other Christian youth work though, which is earnest, sincere and sacrificial, that seems to be popular with young people and certainly relates to their culture, but nevertheless produces few, if any, changed lives. It has no permanent effect on the world in which it takes place, and seems to achieve little of eternal significance.

Why is that?

The answer

The cultural distance between the world of the Bible and the world of our own day should not be minimised, but to tell young people about the God who made them and loves them, in a way that they can understand, demands a close attention to what that God has revealed about himself. Here is the foundation for Christian work with teenagers.

The Bible, however, does not contain a systematic theology of youth. There is no mention of the 'teenager' or the 'youth worker'. Adolescents were not regarded as a significant category of society in the ancient world in the way they are today.

Clearly there are problems of 'cultural transposition' in looking back into the Bible to find guidelines for modern youth work. It is necessary to discover the principles that underlie their practices in order to transfer those principles from their culture and apply them to our own culture. We may not wear phylacteries or write texts on our doorposts (Deut. 6:8–9), but those practices may have expressed an important principle for ancient Judaism which we should not ignore (and for which we must find contemporary applications).

For this search to be successful it must be expectant and humble. We come to the Bible expecting to learn from it and willing to learn from it. It must be allowed to speak for itself – however uncomfortable, unfashionable, or alien its voice may sound at first.

It is often those things with which we are least comfortable that have most to teach us, because they pave the way to new insights and do not merely reinforce our present attitudes and opinions. This is an important principle of study if we are to hear God speaking to us through the Bible. Otherwise we may peer deep into the well of truth, only to see a reflection of our own faces. This principle has other important implications too.

For example, it will guard us from despising the youth work of older generations. There can be a dangerous contemporary arrogance which looks down on earlier patterns of youth ministry as though God never guided or spoke to our predecessors, and has reserved his ultimate revelation on this matter for today. The archives in the CYFA office contain photographs of 'CYFA Rallies' at the Royal Albert Hall in the 1970s, where the singing is led by several hundred teenagers playing six-string classical guitars conducted by a gentleman wearing a white suit (who is now an

Anglican bishop!). We would be appalled to put on an event like that today, but it was appropriate then. And what will they be saying in twenty years time about our youth work today? Don't despise the youth work of older generations.

This approach will also keep us from making the interpretation of the Bible an intellectual achievement. It is important to study the Bible carefully, particularly when there is such a large cultural gap between adolescence in the ancient world and adolescence today. But God doesn't reveal his truth to the learned and conceal it from the simple. Rather the reverse. We set out to master the Bible in order to be mastered by it. The will of God is not so much discerned by an understanding of such theological niceties as 'the new hermeneutic', 'dynamic equivalence', or 'redaction criticism', as by our willingness to obey him whatever the cost.

This humble and expectant approach to the Bible will avoid the attitude of arrogant detachment, which sees the biblical material as an interesting basis for discussion, but no more than that. Such an attitude resorts to subjectivism ('I think . . . I feel . . . In my experience . . .') at any point where the Bible contradicts previous opinions and prejudices. 'Feeling' has very little to contribute in the search for God's remedy for the church's youth decay.

So we begin this search humbly and expectantly in the pages of the Bible.

The God of all ages

The ancient world knew nothing of the 'teenager', and Eli bringing up Samuel in the temple must be virtually the only biblical account of a 'youth worker'.

If that really was the forerunner of our youth groups, it is particularly encouraging. It has one member, who keeps falling asleep. It has one leader, who is antique (although admittedly a valuable one), and half blind. And they meet in church, without any other facilities at all. Your group's not so bad after all, is it?

But actually the Bible has a great deal to say about God's dealings with children and young people. In fact, the Bible is insistent that God is the God of the child. This is particularly striking because children counted for little in ancient society.

With high rates of infant mortality, the child had few rights and low status. Children were a marginalised and disadvantaged social category. When Matthew records Jesus' feeding miracles, he writes: 'The number of those who ate was about five thousand men, besides women and children' (Mt. 14:21), and 'The number of those who ate was four thousand, besides women and children' (Mt. 15:38).

This reflects the lack of social significance of the women and children. However, the Bible also contains several indications of a different attitude. In Leviticus 27 there is a valuation of persons 'vowed to the LORD': a male from twenty years up to sixty years old was valued at fifty shekels of silver (a woman was valued at thirty), while a male from five years to twenty years old was worth twenty shekels (and a girl ten). From one month to five years old a boy was valued at just five shekels and a girl at three shekels. This suggests that Jewish society did accord a certain status to the child, even if a limited one. Children, and particularly sons, were God's gift to a man and a sign of his blessing:

> Sons are a heritage from the LORD,
> children a reward from him.

> Like arrows in the hands of a warrior
> are sons born in one's youth.
> Blessed is the man whose quiver is full of them.
> They will not be put to shame
> when they contend with their enemies in the gate.
> (Ps. 127:3–5)

Similarly, the 'fatherless' are a category to be protected by law, along with the stranger, the widow and the poor (Ex. 22:21–24). Orphans were to be cared for by God's people, in an age which tended to exploit them.

The Old Testament also suggests that an index of what is happening to a society is provided by what is happening to its young. The violent death of small children is an indication of extreme calamity (Nah. 3:10), or the worst of curses on an enemy: 'Happy is he who repays you for what you have done to us – he who seizes your infants and dashes them against the rocks' (Ps. 137:8, 9).

The happiness and well-being of the young are signs that God has visited his people: 'The city streets will be filled with boys and girls playing there' (Zech. 8:5); 'How attractive and beautiful they will be! Grain will make the young men thrive, and new wine the young women' (Zech. 9:17).

One of the most abominable of all the Canaanite practices was the worship of Molech, involving children being burnt alive. Any Israelite (or any stranger living in Israel) who offered a child to Molech was to be put to death and to be cut off from among the people (Lev. 20:1–5). The very lowest point of degradation for the people of Israel would be when they themselves resorted to eating their own children (Lev. 26:29). In the blessings and cursings set before Israel in Deuteronomy 28, the ultimate consequence of rejecting God is that the nation will be afflicted to the point where women will eat their children and even their afterbirths, jealously guarding them from other members of their family. This is a horrific picture of the lowest depths to which the life of a nation could sink.

The welfare of the young was an important factor in Israelite society because God dealt with the young. He begins his dealings with people even before birth. In Psalm 139 the writer praises God:

> For you created my inmost being;
> you knit me together in my mother's womb.
> I praise you because I am fearfully
> and wonderfully made;
> your works are wonderful,
> I know that full well.
> My frame was not hidden from you
> when I was made in the secret place.
> When I was woven together in the
> depths of the earth,
> your eyes saw my unformed body.
> All the days ordained for me
> were written in your book
> before one of them came to be. (Ps. 139:13–16)

In certain cases this dealing was specifically related to later ministry. Jeremiah's call to be a prophet began with God telling him, 'Before I formed you in the womb I knew you, before you were born I set you apart; I appointed you as a prophet to the nations' (Jer. 1:5). Samuel was consecrated to God before conception and grew up 'in the presence of the LORD' (1 Sam. 2:21), developing 'in stature and in favour with the LORD and with men' (1 Sam. 2:26). Samson was also dedicated before birth and the LORD blessed him in his boyhood (Judg. 13:24). Moses was 'no ordinary child' (Acts

7:20). The angel prophesied of John the Baptist that he would be 'filled with the Holy Spirit even from birth' (Lk. 1:15). The angel who appeared to the shepherds announced that Jesus, even as an infant a few hours old, was 'Saviour' (Lk. 2:11).

Right of access

The Bible teaches that God can relate to and deals with a person from the moment of conception (and before). It also makes clear that children have their own right of access to God. The disciples tried to prevent over-enthusiastic mothers from wasting Jesus' time with blessing their children (Mt. 19:13–15). Their response was typical of their age: it was the parents (and particularly the fathers) who should receive the benefits of Jesus' teaching. Then it could be passed on to the rest of the family at home. But Jesus contradicted this: 'Let the little children come to me, and do not hinder them', he said; 'for the kingdom of heaven belongs to such as these.' Jesus went against the attitudes and assumptions of his day in asserting the right of children to their own access to God and to their own authentic spiritual experiences.

As far as physical and mental abilities go, there is a growth and development through infancy, childhood, youth and into adulthood, which can be seen as a progression and an improvement. It is not so with the spirit; the child's perception of God may be very different from the adult's, but it is not inferior.

'You have set your glory above the heavens. From the lips of children and infants you have ordained praise', wrote the psalmist (Ps. 8:1–2), and Jesus quoted that psalm when the chief priests and scribes were indignant at the children crying out, 'Hosanna to the

Son of David!' in the temple during his entry into Jerusalem (Mt. 21:15–16). When lamenting the reluctance of his contemporaries to believe in him, Jesus declared, 'I praise you, Father, Lord of heaven and earth, because you have hidden these things from the wise and learned, and revealed them to little children. Yes, Father, for this was your good pleasure' (Mt. 11:25–26).

It may well be that Jesus' use of the term 'little children' in Matthew's Gospel refers to his followers, Christian disciples, but there is strong biblical evidence that children do have a special ability to apprehend God. When asked who was the greatest in the kingdom of heaven, Jesus brought a child before the disciples and told them that unless they became like children they would never even enter the kingdom of heaven. It was the person who humbled himself like a child who was the greatest in that kingdom (Mt. 18:1–4).

There are qualities natural to children (which adults must take the trouble to imitate) that equip them for an immediate access to God. Their helplessness and dependence are spiritual examples for adults.

Where the ancient world looked down on childhood, Jesus advised his followers not to adopt that attitude. R.V.G. Tasker has commented that he had 'an affectionate regard for children which was unique among teachers and writers of the ancient world'. (But this was not mere affection. His attitude was based on theological truth.)

This truth is more than a simple glorification of childhood innocence. Authentic spiritual experience is the right of every age. There is not a progression from the inferior and the infantile to the superior and the adult. While we are encouraged to be mature in our understanding and our faith, we are also warned not to despise the faith of the young. Indeed, if there is any hierarchy of spiritual experience, Jesus would seem to suggest that the order is the reverse of what we would expect. We are to learn valuable spiritual truths from the young '. . . for the kingdom of heaven belongs to such as these' (Mt. 19:14).

The Bible certainly does not give us any warrant to look down on old age either. It contradicts the ancient world's low estimate of childhood without contradicting their high respect for the old. 'Rise in the presence of the aged, show respect for the elderly and revere your God. I am the LORD' (Lev. 19:32). The New Testament says nothing to reduce the force of this command.

The God of the Bible is a God of all human ages. The ability of the human spirit to experience its creator is not limited by the simplicity of childhood, nor by the frailty of old age. So we can be encouraged to extend our search for the Bible's teaching specifically on adolescence knowing that God understands young people, values them, reveals himself to them, and relates to them in a completely appropriate way.

The God of youth

We have already seen from Leviticus 27 that there was a probationary period for the young Jew that extended beyond childhood. It was only when they were twenty years old that the full value was put on a man or a woman. Jesus went up with his parents to the temple at Jerusalem when he was twelve (Lk. 2:41–52), but it is clear even in that passage, that the years which followed were a period of development towards full adulthood: 'Then he went down to Nazareth with them and was obedient to them. But his mother treasured all these things in her heart. And Jesus grew in wisdom and stature, and in favour with God and men' (Lk. 2:51, 52).

So the Bible does not regard children as adults from their thirteenth birthdays, whatever their official social status and whatever the young people themselves may think! It describes Josiah as 'still young' in the eighth year of his reign, when he was sixteen (2 Chr. 34:1–3). There is a category of 'young men' in the Old and New Testaments distinguished from other age groups: '. . . on the children in the street and on the young men gathered together; both husband and wife will be caught in it, and the old, those weighed down with years' (Jer. 6:11; see also Joel 2:28).

In Titus 2 Paul has instructions for the 'older men', the 'older women', the 'younger women' and the 'younger men' (verses 2–6). John twice addresses the three categories of 'dear children', 'fathers' and 'young men' (1 Jn. 2:12–14). In the context these are spiritual categories, but the writer would have derived them from contemporary thinking about human ages. So the people in Paul and John's time thought in terms of 'young' people. There was a period of 'youth' in biblical culture.

It may be that there is evidence here for a rather longer 'probationary' period than we have in modern adolescence. We think that 'youth' finishes legally at eighteen, or at the latest at twenty-one. They had a rather more extended view. Paul was concerned about Timothy's youth in his epistles to his assistant (1 Tim. 4:12), but from the charge the apostle lays on him Timothy was obviously not an adolescent. For the Romans, the period of adolescence *began* at seventeen and ended at about twenty-eight. Arndt and Gingrich in their New Testament Greek Lexicon suggest that the word *neanias* (the usual New Testament term for 'youth' or 'young man') covers the period from the twenty-fourth to the fortieth year. But some usages (such as Acts 23:16–22) may indicate that it covers a younger period as well.

Although a young person might enter the world of work and labour in his early teens, he was still allowed a moratorium, a space to develop and grow, before taking on the full responsibilities of mature adulthood. How long this period was is not certain, but it would have been equivalent to the experience of adolescence in our own society.

This period was regarded then, as it is today, as a time of probation, of experiment, of trial and error, when a degree of irresponsibility was to be expected, if not commended: 'Be happy, young man, while you are young, and let your heart give you joy in the days of your youth. Follow the ways of your heart and whatever your eyes see' (Ecc. 11:9). The author goes on to warn of God's judgement and the need to remember our creator in the days of our youth.

It was also a time for achievement. The Bible records and commends the successes of many young people. In the history books of the Old Testament (particularly the record of David's career in 1 Samuel) the term 'young man' or 'young men' (Hebrew *naar*) was used particularly for those involved in heroic feats. The Jericho spies were 'young men' (Josh. 6:23). David's own youthfulness was stressed when he slew Goliath (1 Sam. 17:33). There is a long list of those who achieved great things in their youth, including Joseph, Samuel, Samson, Joash, Azariah/Uzziah, Josiah, Esther, Daniel, Hananiah and Mishael – a list we could extend perhaps to the New Testament with the lad who provided his lunch for the feeding of the five thousand in John 6:9, and Paul's nephew who warned the Tribune of the Jewish plot to kill Paul (Acts 23: 16–22).

These youthful achievements show that adolescence is a period when great accomplishments and spiritual leadership are possible. Just as the spiritual experience of the young is not to be relegated below adult spirituality, so young men and women are not to wait until adulthood before they can achieve things for God. When Jeremiah said, 'Ah, Sovereign LORD . . . I do not know how to speak; I am only a child', God replied, 'Do not say, "I am only a child." You must go to everyone I send you to and say whatever I command you' (Jer. 1:6–7).

God still sends the young to speak for him, just as much as he sends adults. How do these biblical examples compare with the responsibilities given to young people in the churches today?

The church does not do youth and children's work in order to guarantee its own future – to ensure a good supply of future adult believers. It is often said that young people are not 'tomorrow's church' but 'today's church'. The reason why young people are the church of today is not stated so often.

We need to encourage our young people and make them feel important. And we do that, not as a patronising concession, nor just because the church is a family and should therefore consist of all ages; but primarily because *God is a God of all ages.* We keep young people in the centre of the church's life because we want to be true to God. Just as distinctions of race or colour or physique or intelligence count for nothing with him, nor do distinctions of age. Every human being is of equal value in his eyes.

So we must not underestimate the spiritual experience and the spiritual potential of the teenager. The Bible suggests that youth is made for heroism. It is our world that insists it is made for pleasure. If we take the Bible seriously, we will look for great spiritual achievements among young people, achievements that will sometimes eclipse those of adults.

Richard Wurmbrand used to tell the story of a boy in the persecuted Romanian church who arrived one day at the gate of a prison camp and asked to see the commandant. When he was allowed into the man's office, he said this:

> Today is Mothers' Day and every year on Mothers' Day I buy my mother a bunch of flowers in the market. But last year my mother was put into your prison for being a Christian and she died there. This year I have no one to give my flowers to – so I have brought them here for you, to give to your wife.

That is the faith that overcomes the world. It is often more powerful in the young than in the old. We should expect a deep spirituality in young people and, if the Bible is a reliable guide, we will not be disappointed. If the Son of God himself passed through the teenage years (although we know virtually nothing about those years in his life), then there is a pattern of perfect relationship with God appropriate to that age.

As the Bible stresses the high value God puts on young people and the high expectations that he has of their spirituality, it also has much to teach us today about evangelism, youth discipling, the church, the family, and patterns of youth work for the local church. We will consider these in the coming chapters.

If we take the Bible seriously, we can see that God does understand the young, and that his word does give us principles for working with them. It is our responsibility to find out what these principles are, and to apply them to our work with our young people.

RESPONSE

1. This chapter is entitled *Gray's Anatomy, Michelin Guide or instruction book?* Which of these best describes the Bible as it relates to youth work? What is a better analogy? If you are working with other leaders, have a brainstorm and discussion about this.
2. Jot down a short summary of what you learned from this chapter. If you meet with other youth leaders, ask them to do the same, and then compare notes.
3. Try reading the whole of Deuteronomy at a sitting (it won't take you nearly as long as you think), and note down what it tells you about children and young people. If that seems like a real struggle, get hold of one of the CDs where the Bible is read out loud, and listen to it on a long car journey. Do the same with one of the gospels, and then do it again with 1 and 2 Timothy and Titus. If you can, ask someone else to do the same, and then sit down with them and a cup of coffee and compare your results. If you are a youth leader, and part of a team of leaders, use this as an activity for your next leaders' meeting.
4. Keep a small notebook, and when you read your Bible, or hear it read, and there is a reference to

children or young people, jot it down in your notebook, preferably copying out the verse.

5. Note down what *you* think the Bible has to say about children and young people. Then use a concordance to check what you have written against Bible verses, and see if they really agree!

Notes

1 *Reaching and Keeping Teenagers*, Peter Brierley, MARC, 1993

2 *The Tide is Running Out*, Peter Brierley, Christian Research, 2000

3 *A Workbook on Reaching and Keeping Tweenagers*, Peter Brierley, Christian Research, 2002

4 *Youth Culture and the Gospel*, Pete Ward, Marshall Pickering, 1992

5 Youth for Christ, 'Into View magazine', Issue 4, Spring 1994

2. Oak Trees or Beansprouts?

Adolescent conversion

Take your pick youth work

Go into any supermarket and you will be besieged by a bewildering display of items. Just how many different varieties of canned tomatoes can there be? Do we really need the choice of eight different sorts of potato?

Youth work is a bit like that. Wherever you look, it is being done differently. The choice is bewildering.

Some models of youth ministry focus on improving the 'deal' that young people get from the authorities. Others focus on investing huge amounts of time with a small number of young people, being Christ to them. Others concentrate on understanding young people, and producing a youth programme which really scratches where the young people of today (as opposed to yesterday) are itching.

Many of these approaches focus strongly on the young people themselves, but not on a Christian understanding of people. Christ does not teach us to support the personal development of young people so that they may realise their full potential. We are instead to call them to repentance and faith, because only in that way can they begin to realise their full potential.

The first aim of Christian youth work must be to present a young person with the claims of Jesus Christ. In his book *Working with Teenagers,* Nick Aiken writes: 'So what should be our basic aim in working with young people? To challenge them with the message of Christ and to nurture them in the way of Christian discipleship.'[1] It is only by an encounter with the living God that a young person's deepest needs can be met.

Those who represent the church to teenagers will have betrayed them if the young people who pass through their hands have not been confronted with the person of the living Christ.[2]

Jesus teaches that our worst problems lie within our own hearts (Mk. 7:23), but that the solution to those problems does not lie within. We have destroyed a relationship with God that only God can restore. It is an understanding and a trust in what God did for us through the incarnation, crucifixion and resurrection of his Son that sets us free to relate to him. Only in that relationship can a young person – or anyone else – find real freedom and fulfilment. Jesus made the choice clear, and did not conceal the consequences of rejecting God's offer.

> If anyone would come after me, he must deny himself and take up his cross and follow me. For whoever wants to save his life will lose it, but whoever loses his life for me and for the gospel will save it. What good is it for a man to gain the whole world, yet forfeit his soul? Or what can a man give in exchange for his soul? If anyone is ashamed of me and my words in this adulterous and sinful generation, the Son of Man will be ashamed of him when he comes in his Father's glory with the holy angels. (Mk. 8:34–38)

Youth work is not Christian if it is not true to Jesus Christ in facing young people with this gospel and warning them of the consequences of not accepting it. It is this message that distinguishes Christian youth work from secular youth work. If we abandon it, we are discarding the most important contribution that we can make as Christians.

Our society was probably never Christian in any realistic sense of the word. It is certainly not Christian today, because most people do not live their lives under the lordship of Jesus Christ. The Christian response to a non-Christian (or post-Christian) society is to challenge individuals to face Christ's claim to rule. This even comes before the regeneration of the society itself. If Christianity has influenced the history of the human race at all, it has been primarily because of the conversion of individuals. God does not start anywhere else with mankind.

Of course, renewed individuals are called to challenge the presuppositions and structures of society. It is not a choice between the regeneration of individuals or the changing of society. Both must go together. But whenever Christianity has failed to convert individuals, it has quickly ceased to have any long-term effects upon the culture.

So Christian youth work must focus on the individual, but it is not individualistic. Christianity teaches the dignity and freedom of the individual. We are each of great value, a value quite independent of our looks, our achievements, our popularity, even our own estimates of ourselves.

Unlike much current teaching, Christianity does not encourage a quest to find our true 'self'. The idea of the real inner 'me', whom I need to recognise, acknowledge, affirm and release to be myself, is not Christian at all.

It is a Greek idea which makes us out to be onions: if we peel off enough skins, eventually we will discover the real identity within. But what if, when we finally discard the last skin, there is nothing left?

Our cultural emphasis on the self is summarised in the Bible by a single short word: sin. There is not a real, true self lurking within young people which we should be helping them to discover. They discover their real selves by submission to God, who first shaped them within the womb and who remakes them in Christ into the individuals they were really meant to be. We do not find ourselves; we are made by God.

That is the Christian approach to the search for personal identity. We discover our own identity as we choose to enter a relationship with our maker. As we receive God's Spirit and have God's law written upon our hearts, so we find out who we are. The biblical injunction is not to 'find' myself, but to 'lose' myself (Mk. 8:35).

Let's get biblical

We see this demonstrated by the delicate balance the Bible maintains between the individual and the community. The solidarity of the individual with his family, his tribe and his nation is stressed. The covenant with Abraham, although made with an individual, is a covenant with the nation:

> I will establish my covenant as an everlasting covenant between me and you and your descendants after you for the generations to come, to be your God and the God of your descendants after you. (Gen. 17:7)

In terms of the agreement with Abraham as an individual, this was a meaningless promise, because its fulfilment was several centuries away. But Abraham would live on in his descendants, and his descendants were already present in him.

This helps to explain verses which seem particularly hard for us, such as God declaring to Moses that he 'punishes the children and their children for the sin of the fathers to the third and fourth generation' (Ex. 34:7). There would have been no discrepancy or discord in the minds of the Israelites between the beautiful early verses of Psalm 137, lamenting the captivity in Babylon – 'By the rivers of Babylon we sat and wept when we remembered Zion' – and the apparently dreadful final verse about '. . . he who seizes your infants and dashes them against the rocks'. We probably find such thoughts horrific, but it would be a contradiction for Israel to wish for the destruction of their enemies, the Babylonians, and to leave the Babylonian children to live on, because the Babylonians still lived in their children.

This corporate dimension to all human life is present in the New Testament as well. Paul and Silas had no hesitation in telling the Philippian jailer that if he believed in the Lord Jesus he would be saved *with his household* (Acts 16:31).

We have lost our sense of this corporate involvement with one another, our sense of identity with our families and our nation. But it is not the Bible which is odd in its sense of communal solidarity. It is we who are odd in our overdeveloped individualism. We are a bunch of individualists, not a team. This has many applications to youth ministry which we will need to consider in time. But first we must look at the other side of the coin.

The Bible also sets out a clear case for individual responsibility. One application of this is that Christian youth work must start with the individual, although, in the light of what we have been saying about the corporate nature of our faith, it cannot end there.

The balance is apparent in the covenant God made with the house of David. When David planned to build the temple, God sent the prophet Nathan to him to say:

> When your days are over and you rest with your fathers, I will raise up your offspring to succeed you, who will come from your own body, and I will establish his kingdom . . . I will establish the throne of his kingdom for ever . . . my love will never be taken away from him, as I took it away from Saul, whom I removed from before you. Your house and your kingdom shall endure for ever before me; your throne shall be established for ever. (2 Sam. 7:12–16)

But, when God spoke later to Solomon about the building of the temple it was clear that the promise to David had not removed from Solomon his own freedom and individuality:

> The word of the LORD came to Solomon: 'As for this temple you are building, if you follow my decrees, carry out my regulations and keep all my commands and obey them, I will fulfil through you the promise I gave to David your father.' (1 Kgs. 6:11–13)

The conditional promise never removed the freedom of the following generations. They were still free to reject what God had promised to their fathers. Rejection was simple: all they had to do was to refuse to obey God's commands. At the dedication of the temple, it was clear that Solomon had understood the conditions. He specifically reminded God of the words of his promise to David: 'You shall never fail to have a man to sit before me on the throne of Israel, if only your sons are careful in all they do to walk before me as you have done' (1 Kgs. 8:25; see also Ps. 89:29–39).

It would seem that the children did not have to opt into the covenant, but they were never counted in against their choice. Here is the delicate balance between corporate solidarity, whereby God deals with a whole community through the generations, and individual responsibility, where each person must answer for his own sin. As our young people emerge into adulthood, we should be challenging them to make their own choice and to take responsibility for their own spiritual lives.

New covenant

That was about the old covenant. But now there's a new one, and the new covenant stresses individual accountability *and* personal relationship. The context of the well-known passage about the new covenant in Jeremiah 31 highlights this shift in emphasis:

> 'In those days people will no longer say,
>
> "The fathers have eaten sour grapes,
> and the children's teeth are set on edge."
>
> 'Instead, everyone will die for his own sin; whoever eats sour grapes – his own teeth will be set on edge.
>
> 'The time is coming,' declares the LORD,
> 'when I will make a new covenant
> with the house of Israel . . .
>
> 'No longer will a man teach his neighbour,
> or a man his brother, saying, "Know the LORD,"
> because they will all know me,
> from the least of them to the greatest . . .

'For I will forgive their wickedness
and will remember their sins no more.' (Jer. 31:29–34)

The contrast is between an old covenant, which dealt with the whole people of God corporately, and a new covenant, under which individuals will experience a personal relationship with God through the forgiveness of sins. Religious experience will no longer be mediated through the whole people – each man teaching his neighbour, saying, 'Know the LORD,' but every individual 'from the least of them to the greatest' will have his own experience of God, because he will have God's law written within him, written upon his heart.

The same vision inspired Joel:

'And afterwards,
I will pour out my Spirit on all people.
Your sons and daughters will prophesy,
your old men will dream dreams,
your young men will see visions.
Even on my servants, both men and women,
I will pour out my Spirit in those days.' (Joel 2:28–29)

No longer would there be an elite who experienced God's Spirit on behalf of the nation (prophets, priests and kings). The Spirit would now become the property of all God's people, so that any individual can have a personal experience of God, and so discover their individual identity.

This individualism is confirmed by Jesus' warning that family unity will sometimes be shattered by faith in him (Mt. 10:35–36; Lk. 12:52; 21:16). The parable of the prodigal son focuses on a relationship of free individuals, and in its context in Luke 15 (where it is preceded by the parables of the lost sheep and the lost coin) highlights the importance of the individual to

God: 'I tell you that in the same way there will be more rejoicing in heaven over one sinner who repents than over ninety-nine righteous persons who do not need to repent' (Lk. 15:7).

We have already considered how his teaching on childhood and youth hinged on the right of every individual of whatever age to have immediate access to God, contradicting the assumptions of the ancient world about childhood. When questioned about a man blind from birth (Jn. 9:1–3), Jesus denied that his blindness should be attributed to his parents' sin, again rejecting his contemporaries' assumptions about corporate solidarity.

We can apply this to the adolescent quest for identity. The individual is given his identity by commitment to, and relationship with, God. It is by decision and by commitment that individual identity is determined. Young people do not need to engage in post-modern activities in order to find their real selves. There is no discovery of identity to be made by inward contemplation or soul-searching. By submission to God the individual brings him- or herself to the point where they can learn from God, and God can bring them into reality.

It was only when David's sons committed themselves to walk before God as David had walked before God that the covenant became a reality for them. They claimed for themselves that relationship which allowed God to do, for them, all the good he had promised their forefather. That was the moment at which they began to realise their full potential.

When a young person wants to step out of the crowd – to be 'himself' rather than just another member of a group – that is the moment at which God can meet him. It is only in relationship to God that he can find his full individuality. That relationship is discovered by exercising the will to choose: to choose to make a general and corporate offer from the creator a personal one. This choice enables a person to grow up. People find their identities by exercising choice.

Cross examination

It is this choice that Christian youth work must be offering young people, and the cross of Christ will always be at the centre of it. The cross challenges young people to choose. It shows them the enormous love that God has for them and the very high price that he was prepared to pay to forgive them. 'But God demonstrates his own love for us in this: While we were still sinners, Christ died for us' (Rom. 5:8).

The crisis of self-esteem, which is such a common experience in adolescence, is not satisfied by repeated and well-meaning assurances like, 'You're not nearly as bad as you think you are.' Every time a friend says that to a depressed young person, a little voice inside wants to say, 'If only you knew me, you'd know I am really far worse.'

The cross of Jesus provides a quite different answer. It says, 'Actually, you know, you are much worse than you think you are – so bad that Jesus had to die an appalling death to bear the dreadful separation that your evil has made between you and God. But God loves you so much, just as you are here and now, that he sent Jesus to die that death for you. And Jesus has done that. God values you that much. And now he offers you new life for Jesus' sake.'

The cross offers new life. But it also makes clear the starkness of the choice. When Jesus invited his followers to take up their cross and follow him, they would have been in no doubt as to what he meant. If you saw someone carrying a cross in first-century Palestine, you did not see that person again. He was on a one-way journey to the grave. Jesus meant the end of one sort of self-centred life and the start of a completely different life. So Paul wrote:

> I have been crucified with Christ and I no longer live, but Christ lives in me. The life I live in the body, I live by faith in the Son of God, who loved me and gave himself for me. (Gal. 2:20)

The cross is the anchor point for Christian youth work. The cross will guard against our work becoming secular youth work with a nominal religious veneer. Christian youth work is not just youth work with an extra spiritual dimension to it: doing what the Youth Service does, but doing it rather worse because of lack of funding. We are not just a secular youth club which pushes in a 'God slot' because it is being held on church premises. Christian youth work is done first and foremost in obedience to Christ – who told us to make disciples of all nations, and died on the cross so that this might be possible.

The cross will also guard against the temptation to change the gospel when we find that results do not come easily. If Christian youth work aims at the conversion of the individual, and individuals do not get converted, then questions are bound to arise. It is right that they should. But we have already been warned that the message we proclaim will be neither sensational nor popular. 'Jews demand miraculous signs and Greeks look for wisdom,' wrote Paul, 'but we preach Christ crucified: a stumbling-block to Jews and foolishness to Gentiles' (1 Cor. 1:22–23).

The message of the cross will not be popular. It will not normally provoke a massive response. It is right that we should regularly examine our message to check whether we have not added things which need to be shed. Sometimes it is not the gospel that is being rejected, but the ghastly wrapping paper that we have smothered it in. It is essential that these wrappings are regularly and ruthlessly removed.

For example, we like to grade sin so that some sins are much more evil than others. Child abuse would be high up on the list today, but hypocrisy would be way down, and working hard to get rich (very rich) would scarcely get on to the list at all. Such hierarchies of sin are derived from our culture, not from the Bible. They need frequent re-examination.

The final test must be whether our gospel is true to God's revealed will in the Bible, not whether it is making inroads into contemporary society. We can only redefine the gospel to make it truer to the work and teaching of Jesus. Once we start asking questions like 'What's the gospel for young people?' or 'What's the gospel for today's street kids?' we are saying that we want to redefine the gospel to make it more relevant today, or to certain parts of today's society. You cannot actually do that, because the gospel is the gospel. It may be applied in slightly different ways to different people, but the historic truths of the gospel are unchanging. If we attempt to redefine its substance, we are starting on a very dangerous journey.

Evangelism is central to Christian youth work and that means the cross must be central. But a commitment to evangelism and proclaiming the cross will need to be seasoned with a mature understanding of young people, their culture, and the emotional pressures of adolescence.

But we do not talk just about the cross. And we are not saying that the message will be precisely the same, whoever we talk to. The first Christians clearly highlighted certain parts of their message depending on their audience. So, for instance, when talking to Gentiles, 'Jesus is Lord' is emphasised, and when talking to Jewish audiences, 'Jesus is the Christ' is emphasised. There were limits to this variation, but the variation existed. The gospel does not change, but we must vary our presentation of it to meet the cultural situation we are addressing. But there are essentials which cannot be omitted, and there are many cultural accretions which need to be challenged. The gospel can be presented in any way and with any emphasis, providing that the variation lies within New Testament limits.

Power people

'I want everyone to bow their heads and close their eyes. No one is to look. If God has spoken to you tonight . . . and you want to respond to what he has been saying, please raise your hand to God. No one will be looking. This is just between you and him. Just raise your hand to tell him you are willing to do what he wants you to.'

Even as the young evangelist spoke, it struck me that there was one person in the hall that evening who did not need anyone to raise their hands to indicate the state of their hearts. God knew exactly who was responding and who was not. The raised hands were not for his benefit.

Had all eyes been open and every head up, the gesture would have been a public profession of faith – a helpful first step, perhaps, to confessing Christ with their lips. Then it would have been for the benefit of those responding. But the speaker insisted that every head remained bowed and every eye closed. It was his first remark to me after the meeting that revealed the real purpose of the raised hands: 'Did you see the response?' It was for his benefit that those young people had raised their hands. He had been watching (and he had expected me to be watching), because he needed the encouragement of seeing that the gospel worked.

This small incident highlights the weakness of much youth evangelism. We judge it by standards of success or failure, and not by its obedience to God's will. We have allowed ourselves to become besotted with the power images of contemporary youth culture.

So there is an emphasis on gathering together large numbers of young people, so that 'they can see that they are not alone'. There is talk of 'God's young army'. There is an emphasis on 'big name' speakers and the testimonies of well-known individuals, so that the young can see that even the great, the famous and the powerful believe. For some reason, God working in the life of, say, David and Carrie Grant, is a greater thing than God working in your life or mine. No. It's a great thing no matter whose life he's working in!

There is an emphasis on the visible response of large numbers, and this can lead to a complete abuse of evangelistic opportunities. 'I need to get a good response tonight, because that will ensure a full diary for the next year.' That shows not only that some evangelists are consumed by the need to appear successful, but (more worryingly?) that those who invite them, the local church youth leaders and their members, have been taken in by the numbers game as well. So we reverse Paul's dictum that 'we walk by faith and not by sight', and we encourage the young to trust the big battalions rather than the cross of Christ. There is an emphasis on immediacy, excitement, challenge and enthusiasm, so that the answer to doubt is presented as constant exhortation to greater emotional commitment. There is an emphasis on the discipleship of the big event, so that the normal teenage testimony is one of crisis rather than growth. And there is a depersonalisation of youth work, so that we rely on the band, the loud PA, the video wall, and the presentation skills of the evangelist, rather than long-term, quiet, ongoing relationship-building with the young people by a group of committed leaders.

There is a place for big events within Christian youth work. But it is helpful to see them as *special* rather than normal, and as our servants rather than our masters. Many good things can come out of these big events, but we need to have our eyes open as well to the dangers and temptations to shallowness which they present to us. (There is further discussion of the place of the big event in youth ministry in chapter five.)

This shallow pattern of evangelism is often coupled with a disdain for the local church. The outward image of the local church is sometimes caricatured and pilloried by youth speakers, as a way of ingratiating their message to their youthful hearers. Youth workers who earn a cheap laugh and a few more minutes' attention from their audience by launching missiles at a distorted picture of the church just encourage young people to adopt a superior and judgmental attitude towards the church. And this poor image of the church in the minds of young people will cause not just a negative approach to the local congregation, but also a critical approach to *any* church, no matter how good it is. Young people start to see their job as one of changing the church, not of loving it, belonging to it, and being committed to it, warts and all.

As we develop a dissatisfaction with the church we shoot ourselves in the foot, because the church is vital to the long-term survival of young believers. So youth workers who breed dissent are doing the kingdom of God a major disservice, in the short- and long-term.

We will return to this in chapter five, and we will see there that the widespread dissatisfaction among young people with traditional patterns of Christianity may be a very welcome development. But evangelism that does not take the doctrine of the church seriously will do considerable damage, because conversion is not just an individual thing. It must have a strong corporate dimension to it.

The gospel is certainly immediate, exciting and challenging, but this must be tempered with the stark and sober realism of the choice before a young person. The excitement is much more acceptable than the starkness in our age which believes this is what young people want. We must achieve a biblical balance – not neglecting the thrills, but bringing the spills into the open as well. There is no 'Christianity without tears'.

Wising up

There is an interesting distinction between the Bible's teaching about children and its teaching about young people.

With the child there is an emphasis on firm teaching and discipline:

> Train a child in the way he should go,
> and when he is old he will not turn from it. (Prov. 22:6)

> Folly is bound up in the heart of a child,
> but the rod of discipline will drive it far from him.
> (Prov. 22:15)

But with the young person there is the invitation to wisdom, frequently offered in the book of Proverbs.

> Listen, my sons, to a father's instruction;
> pay attention and gain understanding.
> I give you sound learning,
> so do not forsake my teaching.
> When I was a boy in my father's house,
> still tender, and an only child of my mother,
> he taught me and said, 'Lay hold of my words with all your heart;
> keep my commands and you will live.
> Get wisdom, get understanding;
> do not forget my words or swerve from them.
> Do not forsake wisdom, and she
> will protect you;
> love her, and she will watch over you.' (Prov. 4:1–6)

The approach is open; various ways lie before the young person on the threshold of adult life. There are rival offers for his allegiance. It may be the company of evil men (Prov. 1:10–19), or the lure of the seductress (Prov. 5:7), but against these Wisdom makes her appeal.

> Wisdom calls aloud in the street,
> she raises her voice in the public squares;
> at the head of the noisy streets she cries out,
> in the gateways of the city she
> makes her speech:
> 'How long will you simple ones
> love your simple ways?
> How long will mockers delight in mockery
> and fools hate knowledge?
> If you had responded to my rebuke,
> I would have poured out my heart to you
> and made my thoughts known to you.' (Prov. 1:20–23)

The tone is quite different from the Bible's instructions to children – 'Children, obey your parents in the Lord, for this is right' (Eph. 6:1); 'Children, obey your parents in everything, for this pleases the Lord' (Col. 3:20).

There is a recognition of the increasing independence of adolescents, of their right to make up their own minds, and of their dignity in exercising freedom of choice as beings made in God's image. To be adult is to make your own choices. The wisdom literature of the Bible presents the young with the fundamental choices of life and pleads with them to choose correctly.

The strong emphasis on 'wisdom' is not to be mistaken for the quest for intellectual achievement. Academic success is one of the false gods of modern western society. Worship of the intellect is quite different from the way of wisdom urged on us in the book of Proverbs. This wisdom involves accepting and appropriating the older generation's advice: 'A wise son heeds his father's instruction, but a mocker does not listen to rebuke' (Prov. 13:1).

This wisdom is not adorned to make it particularly attractive to the young. The starkness of the choice is made abundantly clear: hard work, moral uprightness, discipline, humility, suffering, faithfulness, maturity and discretion are all stressed. But wisdom is also God's gift. The young are not invited to achieve it, but to choose it, to seek it.

> And if you call out for insight
> and cry aloud for understanding,
> and if you look for it as for silver
> and search for it as for hidden treasure,
> then you will understand the fear of the LORD
> and find the knowledge of God.
> For the LORD gives wisdom,

> and from his mouth come
> knowledge and understanding. (Prov. 2:3–6)

It was God who made Daniel and his three colleagues wise (Dan. 1:17). It is God who by the cross has reversed the wisdom of the world (1 Cor. 1:22–25), and now reveals an eternal wisdom through his Spirit (1 Cor. 2:6–10).

The Bible respects young people's aspiration to adulthood and presents the young with a realistic choice. There is no distortion to tip the balance unfairly in one direction. There is a deep respect for the dignity and freedom of the young person. Nothing is concealed.

There is no small print, and there are no hidden clauses, but the urgency of the plea is unmistakable: 'My son, give me your heart and let your eyes keep to my ways' (Prov. 23:26). It is a life-or-death choice upon which every person's ultimate happiness depends.

There is much here to apply directly to modern youth evangelism. Is our evangelism as honest and as free from deceit? Do we show the same respect for the freedom and dignity of our teenage listeners? Do we make the choice as clear and as urgent? Are we sometimes guilty, not of asking too much, but of asking too little of teenagers and so selling them and God short? Are we clear that our appeal springs out of the nature and mind of God, rather than culturally conditioned motives to do with success? Is our offer really the wisdom which made Christ crucified 'the power of God and the wisdom of God' (1 Cor. 1:24)? The cross lies at the centre of this wisdom and must therefore also be the centre of our evangelism.

Grazing out on a Big Mac

We must have a sensitive concern for the young people that we work with, so that we are not tempted to deceive them in any way. We will want to teach them the whole counsel of God with our lives and with our lips.

> Jesus wept? Jesus weeps. He weeps over sheep fed on lollipops . . . He weeps over poor, deceived young people who are falsely taught by enthusiastic preachers that an instant, subjective experience at a special conference will solve all their problems and give them a zippy, automatic, Christian joy for the rest of their lives. Garbage! Lying and devilish garbage – that leads young Christians to despair, to frustration, and to the terrible sense that if things go wrong, God has abandoned them or they have failed.[3]

Our theology must be sufficiently mature to cope with evangelism that fails to get immediate results. In some Christian writing it would appear that evangelism never fails, that it cannot fail. You get this impression from the newsletters sent out from some evangelists. So exaggeration and distortion creep in. Tentative enquirers become converts. Numbers are rounded up. Sensational results are triumphantly proclaimed. We must equip our young people with a theology that can cope with apparent failure.

God does not need statistics to prove his power to save young people. Nor is our own faith built up by that attitude. All too often it is undermined when we compare our first-hand experience of evangelism with the way it is reported in the Christian press. Nor is the non-Christian world impressed with what seems to them like propaganda.

We must take to heart the parable of the sower (Mk. 4:1–20). It was the seed which fell on rocky soil that sprang up with joy. How many of those who hurry to the front at an evangelistic rally are in that category? I was sitting in an evangelistic youth meeting, and the speaker appealed for people to come to the front. Several young people in the row in front of us stood up to go forward. The girl immediately in front of us turned to her neighbour and said, 'Come on, I always go up at these things', and her friend went up as well. Two more spurious statistics. We must beware of equating the act of 'coming forward' with conversion.

We must also beware of working with young people in order to meet our own emotional needs. Some evangelistic programmes for the young insist on a visible response to the gospel, not for the sake of the young people themselves, but for the sake of the leaders who need encouragement in their own ministry.

We must not rob the cross of its power. God is able to save by many or by few. His redemptive work has carried on down the ages. It is not thwarted by the failure of human agencies. He still calls young people to himself through the simple message of forgiveness for Jesus' sake: that they can stop trying to please God in order to earn forgiveness from him, and start rejoicing in the fact that he is already pleased with them just as they are, because Jesus has already paid the price for that forgiveness. 'For Christ died for sins once for all, the righteous for the unrighteous, to bring you to God' (1 Pet. 3:18). It is a message that releases supernatural power into the individual to start to transform her, and through her to start to transform the world.

And this message is going to continue to change human lives, whether we can see it happening, and count it, or not.

Decision time

The number of different models used in the New Testament to describe the character of God's salvation (legal justification, new birth, adoption into a family, washing, from death to life, liberation, accepting lordship, indwelling of God, sacrificial atonement, from darkness to light, turning round, etc.) serves to remind us of the limitations of our own ability to understand God's dealings with people. We are not going to find a clear and total explanation of adolescent conversion.

However, there is a clear balance between God's part in regenerating us and our part in receiving and believing:

> Yet to all who received him, to those who believed in his name, he gave the right to become children of God – children born not of natural descent, nor of human decision or a husband's will, but born of God. (Jn. 1:12–13)

A person cannot will him- or herself to be born. Only God can will it. But God does not do so against the person's will. Much theological ink has been spilt over this point (of the freedom of the human will), and it would not be appropriate to discuss it here, but we must make a distinction between God's action and our response.

The inward spiritual work of regeneration is done by God out of sight. It is an eternal act of the eternal God. The outward profession of conversion is visible and may or may not be genuine. It may come and go, even in an adult. For the teenager this outward profession of conversion presents some particular problems.

The teenager stands between childhood and adulthood. The child is not a free agent. She can only commit to God as much of her time, energy, property, will-power and emotions as she herself is in control of. As she develops greater autonomy and responsibility, so she has to develop a more complete commitment to God. The anomaly of the teenager, or even the adult, trying to live her life with a 'Sunday school' faith is all too familiar.

In some ways the individual who first encounters Christ as an adult has an easier path to tread. Her faith does not have to keep in step with the traumatic upheavals of puberty and adolescence as it first grows and develops. Christians working with children have rightly felt that it is unwise to use highly subjective language about conversion ('Is Jesus real to you?' is a dangerously difficult question for a child to have to answer), and have often preferred to talk about 'following Jesus' rather than 'receiving Jesus'. They also know the dangers of asking a child for an emotionally drastic step of commitment, which makes it very hard for that child to cope with failure and defeat later. How many adults there are who once made some great step of faith as a child and, because it did not 'work', will have nothing more to do with Christ!

Adolescence must be handled just as sensitively. As youth workers we proclaim Christ to our young people and we pray that God will convert them, but we have to direct our attention to the outward and visible human response. On his side, God deals with young people in a way that is entirely appropriate to their age and development (as we saw in chapter one). We do not know exactly what that means for the inward work of regeneration – there is no material in the Bible that gives us specific insight into this – but we must work out what it means for the outward work of conversion.

The young person needs psychological space in which to develop. We need to remember what it was like to be a teenager. The most powerful convictions of one week may have blurred and dimmed by the next. Our most deeply committed young people at one meeting may seem to be distinctly cool at another. As a young person struggles to discover their own identity, we must be very sensitive about confusing that search by trying to hang adult labels upon him, which may satisfy us but are unhelpful to him. On the one hand, we believe passionately that his fundamental need is for a personal experience of the living God, but, on the other hand, we treat him with all the love and sensitivity and maturity that the living God inspires in us.

This may mean allowing a young person to leave a youth fellowship. God allowed his first child, Adam, to disobey him. He did not change the rules when he saw that Adam was about to eat the forbidden fruit. The prodigal son was given his share of the property and allowed to leave the family home. We are less than biblical when we exert great emotional pressure to keep a young person in a fellowship. Perhaps we do it more because we ourselves cannot live with the prospect of failure, than because we are concerned to obey God and to love and respect the individual.

We will need to help our young people constantly to update their faith, to find appropriate expression for it as their own life stage changes. We will be cautious to respect their vulnerability to emotional pressure. The big event and the large crowd can communicate a message that its organisers never intended. The fourteen-year-old girl, whose first steady relationship with a boyfriend has just ended, may be making a completely genuine response to the offer of the friendship of Jesus, but we would be wise to take it with a pinch of gently loving salt. We will want to try to guard her against making a drastic commitment that was never genuine in the first place, and from which she can only later extricate herself by abandoning all contact with the Christian faith.

We will want to reflect on what we are doing when we apply adult methods of evangelism to young people. A stereotyped adult model of conversion does not fit them, so it is unlikely that adult methods of evangelism will meet their needs, but the statistics show very clearly that crusade-style evangelism *will* prove to be a youth event. The organisers have no excuse for surprise when an age-analysis shows that a very high percentage of those who came forward were teenagers. We must therefore give careful thought to adequate youth discipleship and follow-up at such events.

It must be recognised that the conversion of a young person is not just an individual crisis (a personal decision on a particular evening at a particular meeting). It also has a gradual and a corporate dimension to it. Some youth workers like to think in terms of a 'four-year conversion', an extended process in the life of a young person in which he comes from darkness to light. At some point – perhaps at the beginning, perhaps at the end – God regenerates that person. We have no infallible insight into when that may be in any individual case. At some point the young person himself professes conversion. That may or may not coincide with God's work of regeneration. But along the way these things happen.

It is the task of the youth leader to care prayerfully for the young person through all those years. In one sense the call to conversion never ends in the life of the believer. The Holy Spirit will continue to lay claim to fresh areas of our lives throughout our earthly pilgrimage. In another sense there is only one moment in which each individual passes from death to life, as God through his Spirit enters our hearts.

It is more helpful to young people to view conversion in the light of this gradual process, than to put too much emphasis on the crisis decision. The challenge to decide must be faithfully made – the cross demands that – but we must be reluctant to hang 'saved' or 'unsaved' labels too hastily around our young people's necks. It is sometimes easier (and more helpful) to ask the question: 'Is he or she spiritually hungry?' or: 'Which way is he or she facing at the moment?' than to ask the question: 'Is he or she saved?' We are desperate for the answer to the latter question (and rightly so), but God does not always trust us with it. We may have to persevere with the faithful work of an under-shepherd and leave the eventual outcome of the matter to God.

If it is a gradual process, it is also a corporate one. The church, whether we like it or not, is a part of the gospel. God calls us into community. This is especially relevant to the teenager. It is notoriously hard for a young person under sixteen to hold an independent set of beliefs. He or she needs to be part of a tribe.

We put unknown pressures on the forming personality if we expect a young person to reject identification with other teenagers for the sake of Christ. Somehow or other we must provide a community of faith in which the young person can live. In a frontier situation, this may be the foremost obstacle to evangelism. It may be necessary to look across denominational boundaries, across social and cultural barriers, even across a considerable geographical distance, but some sort of acceptable Christian fellowship must be found. If we neglect this corporate aspect of adolescent conversion, we will seriously jeopardise our youth evangelism.

The test is time

Young people need time and space as they grow up. They need to be protected from the evangelist or the youth worker who sees them as statistics. They are eager to get up out of their seats and come down to the front at rallies and crusades, but, when they do, they need to meet adults with mature theology and a sympathetic understanding of youth. They must be allowed to take as much time as they need to make their own genuine response to God. We want them to hit the track, but at their own pace.

Youth leaders need great maturity. Emerson said that 'the lesson of life is to believe what the years and centuries say against the hours'. It is certainly the lesson of youth work to believe what the years say against the weeks. All too familiar are the mushroom youth fellowships that spring up and flourish, only to wither and vanish again in a year or two. Many adult Christians today look back on a flourishing youth fellowship during their teenage years and wonder what has become of most of their contemporaries. What we want instead is young people who are still going on strong in the years to come.

> The bottom line is 'Where will my kids be five to ten years from now? Is our church preparing them to be Christian leaders?' Good discipleship involves developing a ministry that lasts.[4]

Youth workers need great wisdom. Francis Bacon observed that all that is weighty in history sinks to the bottom of the river where it cannot be seen, while straw and stubble rise to the top. So it is in youth work. We must look beneath the surface. The wise worker is not over-impressed by numbers, by chorus singing, by the 'atmosphere' of a youth meeting, or by young people's own estimates of their spiritual maturity. He or she will pray for that God-given gift of discernment to see deeper into their lives and into their real spiritual needs.

Looking into a river, you may have to make a conscious effort to cut out the surface reflection in order to see the depths. Sometimes in youth work it is necessary deliberately to put surface impressions on one side in order to perceive real spiritual needs. If we love the young people we work with, we will pray for the ability to see below their surfaces. We will not be content to take them at face value.

As we have considered this picture of adolescent conversion, we have drawn some conclusions for youth evangelism along the way, but the main question remains: how then is the gospel best communicated to young people? Answering that question will raise wider issues than just evangelism, so we will deal with it in a separate chapter. In particular we will see that the line between evangelising (outreach) and discipling (teaching) is far from clear.

RESPONSE

1. Choose three young people whom you know well. Think carefully and deeply about each one and note down any details that you have noticed about their spiritual progress in the last six months. It does not matter if they're not

professing to be Christians – just note down what progress you perceive they are making towards the Christian faith. When you have done that, pray specifically for them, keep the notes you have made, and do the same exercise again in another six months.

2. The cross is at the centre of our message, and informs our methods of Christian youth work. It is the epitome of self-giving, sacrificial love. It shows us the seriousness of our sin, and, while apparently a place of great weakness and defeat, is actually a place of great power and victory. How should these facts affect the way that we go about our youth work?

   Think this through, write something down, and if appropriate, discuss what you have written with your other youth leaders.

3. Think back to the last two or three events that you took (or could have taken) your young people to. (Or you could think back to your last couple of youth group meetings.) How were they handled? How did they display wisdom in the way that they handled the emotions of the teenagers? In what ways did they recognise the *process* involved in adolescent conversion? If the arguments in this chapter are valid, in what ways could the meetings be improved? If you are reviewing meetings for which you have responsibility, note down practical steps that you could take.

Notes

1 *Working with Teenagers*, Nick Aiken, Marshall Pickering, 1988
2 *From Maintenance to Mission: Towards the Conversion of England*, Paul Simmons, Grove Books Ltd., 1995
3 *Flirting with the World*, John White, Hodder & Stoughton, 1982
4 *The Youth Builder*, Jim Burns, Harvest House, 1988

3. It's Life to Life

Working with young people (i)

No new problem

Just how are we supposed to pass on the faith to the next generation?

It is not a new question. In fact the problem of passing on the faith to the next generation has always tested the people of God. It is dealt with at length in the Bible, and is in fact one of the major themes of the Old Testament.

We find there not only a recognition of the problem, but also powerful teaching on how to solve it effectively. It is teaching that speaks directly to us today, thousands of years later. We tend to overlook what it is saying because we have to transfer Old Testament teaching from its cultural setting to our own. As it stands, much of it seems irrelevant – about as helpful as an ashtray on a motorbike. But it is a task worth doing, and it is easier than we might expect. In fact, the Old Testament starts right where we are in this matter.

The spiritual realities of one generation will often be remote and unreal to their offspring:

> The people served the LORD throughout the lifetime of Joshua and of the elders who outlived him and who had seen all the great things the LORD had done for Israel . . .
>
> After that whole generation had been gathered to their fathers, another generation grew up, who knew neither the LORD nor what he had done for Israel. (Judg. 2:7, 10)

The same tale is repeated many times. God would act powerfully at one stage in the nation's history, but memories quickly grew dim and the reality of faith faded as a new generation arose.

From the outset this danger had been taken into account. The religious life of the Israelites was impregnated with a concern to communicate faith effectively from one generation to the next. The purpose of circumcision was that it should be a sign of the covenant to future generations. At eight days old the Israelite male received in his body a powerful and permanent communication about the faith from the previous generation (Gen. 17:9–14).

The whole religious life of Israel was organised to make the young ask questions. The various religious customs and festivals that the Jews had to keep in Canaan were not just quaint, or even downright peculiar, reminders of their religious past. Nor were they just teaching opportunities for a father to lecture his children on the faith. They were vivid *enactments* of the past that were certain to cause the young to ask questions.

> And when your children ask you, 'What does this ceremony mean to you?' then tell them, 'It is the Passover sacrifice to the LORD, who passed over the houses of the Israelites in Egypt and spared our homes when he struck down the Egyptians.' (Ex. 12:26–27)

Animal sacrifice, particularly of a lamb which had been living with the family for a week, would inevitably provoke indignant questioning from younger members of the family. Imagine having the dog put down to celebrate some major holiday today! One cannot deny the vividness of the communication.

The emphasis falls not on the father's teaching, but on the child's questioning and then the father's replying. This was the *purpose* of the nation's religious practices: 'In the future, when your son asks you, "What is the meaning of the stipulations, decrees and laws the LORD our God has commanded you?" tell him . . .' (Deut. 6:20–21).

Throughout the first five books of the Bible there is this passionate concern that the next generation should know the Lord. They saw the problem of 'youth decay' and were concerned to prevent it right from the start, with a kind of spiritual flossing and mouthwash:

> Only be careful, and watch yourselves closely so that you do not forget the things your eyes have seen or let them slip from your heart as long as you live. Teach them to your children and to their children after them. Remember the day you stood before the LORD your God at Horeb, when he said to me, 'Assemble the people before me to hear my words so that they may learn to revere me as long as they live in the land and may teach them to their children.' (Deut. 4:9–10)

This determination had a deep effect on the religious life of Israel, and it challenges us to examine the life of our own churches. Do they show as great a desire to communicate the faith to the younger generation in a living way? We may think that circumcision and animal sacrifice are quaint or barbaric, but have we found equally vivid means of communication? Can we really say the words of Psalm 78?

> We will not hide them from their children;
> we will tell the next generation
> the praiseworthy deeds of the LORD,
> his power, and the wonders he has done.
> He decreed statutes for Jacob
> and established the law in Israel,
> which he commanded our forefathers
> to teach their children,
> so that the next generation would know them,
> even the children yet to be born,
> and they in turn would tell their children.
> Then they would put their trust in God
> and would not forget his deeds
> but would keep his commands. (Ps. 78:4–7)

The challenge is not only the deep concern expressed here. It is also the effectiveness of the communication. As we have seen, the emphasis fell on provoking response as much as on simple telling. Moreover, the faith was communicated across the generation gap not just by specialised religious instruction, but in the normal patterns of everyday living.

> These commandments that I give you today are to be upon your hearts. Impress them on your children. Talk about them when you sit at home and when you walk along the road, when you lie down and when you get up. (Deut. 6:6–7)

Life-to-life

The people of Israel were not communicating just theological propositions; they were communicating a whole way of life. The only proper medium for such communication was life itself. The faith had to be lived out. Just speaking about it was not good enough. Their faith had to be immediately relevant to everyday living, and it had to be seen to be relevant.

The biblical faith was always communicated as a 'culture', a total way of life, in the context of personal relationships and shared experiences. Faith has to be experienced as a life-commitment by adults who act as models to the young. It has to be communicated in both concrete and abstract form, through adult modelling and through verbal communication.

'The youth leader is not primarily a talker or organiser. He is a model, a person who by the power of his Christian example motivates dedication to Jesus Christ.'[1]

The young had to experience the truth of the faith in the lives of the older members of the people of God, as well as listening to the propositions of the faith on the lips of this older generation. The people of Israel were to teach their young as they sat at home and as they walked by the way, as they lay down and when they got up. Our testimony to a conversion experience years ago is not as helpful for a young person as our present experience of relating the faith to the problems of life here and now.

So we have not stumbled upon some quaint characteristics of Israelite family life when we study the wearing of phylacteries or the writing of texts from the Law on the doorway. These practices sprang from the two verses which follow the passage in Deuteronomy 6. The Israelites were to teach God's commands diligently to their children in everyday life: 'Tie them as symbols on your hands and bind them on your foreheads. Write them on the door-frames of your houses and on your gates' (Deut. 6:8–9). Like circumcision and animal sacrifice, this shows the same compulsion to communicate clearly to the young the fact that the Lord is a God relevant to every aspect of every human being's life. So life itself has to be the medium for that communication.

Christian parents must keep the vertical dimension dominant in their practising of their faith within the family. It is no good becoming 'product orientated' in our parenting – trying to live out our Christian lives in order to preach to our children. No one is quicker to detect our hypocrisy (and to resent it) than our own children. Each of us must walk as closely with our God as we can in our families, and let the children draw their own conclusions (see chapter six).

There is a principle here which has a wider application than religious instruction within the family. Jesus instructed his disciples by living alongside them and inviting them to share his life as well as listen to his words. When he first called the twelve, he appointed them primarily to 'be with him' (Mk. 3:14).

And the disciples understood the importance of this life-to-life discipling because, when they chose a successor for Judas Iscariot, Peter stated the criterion on which he should be selected:

> Therefore it is necessary to choose one of the men who have been with us the whole time the Lord Jesus went in and out among us, beginning from John's baptism to the time when Jesus was taken up from us. For one of these must become a witness with us of his resurrection. (Acts 1:21–22)

It was a long-term exposure to the life of Jesus that determined the choice of Matthias to take the place of Judas.

The ministry of Jesus, however, raises a particularly interesting question: when was he evangelising and when was he discipling the twelve disciples?

It is not a distinction we can easily make. Clearly the process was a continuous one and the method was consistent – he lived alongside them and opened his life to them. The medium of communication was not just the spoken word; it was the lived life which, although it included a great many spoken words, was not restricted to them.

Neither evangelism (the communication of the faith to the outsider) nor discipling (the building up in the faith of the convert) will be effective unless we apply this clear biblical principle. The search for effective programmes will fail. In God's service there are only effective people.

We need to note some significant features of Jesus' method. First, there was an extended time involved. Jesus' instruction of the twelve was no crash course, like the final panic before an examination. It had begun before he formally called the twelve of them (they already belonged to a group who were following him, Lk. 6:13), and it continued until the crucifixion and even afterwards. It relied on an extended period of low-key communication, not on a brief period of intense communication – more of a slow cooker than a microwave.

Second, there was a high degree of commitment and intimacy involved. Even though one of the twelve disciples was going to betray him, he made a clear distinction between them and the wider circles of his followers: 'He did not say anything to them without using a parable. But when he was alone with his own disciples, he explained everything' (Mk. 4:34). He lived with them and gave himself to them. Jesus had a quite extraordinary commitment to a small and fairly motley group of people.

Third, there was a clear focus in Jesus' method. While he must have touched the lives of a great number of people, he was content to make a significant impact on the lives of just a few. This aspect of Jesus' work has been widely ignored in Christian youth work, and it is one to which we will return. But first there is some more to say about this whole principle of communication.

Jesus' ministry with the apostles cannot by itself provide the normal pattern for Christian youth work. Clearly his ministry was unique and the twelve apostles are a special case. So we cannot just argue directly from the way Jesus worked with the twelve to the way that we should work with young people today.

We see, however, the same pattern emerging in the rest of the New Testament. Paul wrote to the Thessalonians: 'We loved you so much that we were delighted to share with you not only the gospel of God but our lives as well, because you had become so dear to us' (1 Thes. 2:8). Like Jesus, Paul travelled with a small band of companions with whom he shared his life. When he was separated from them, he suffered great distress (see, for example, 2 Tim. 4:9–22 or 2 Cor. 2:12, 13).

Paul communicated the faith life-to-life and the epistles show that this principle was well understood. Paul wrote, 'Follow my example, as I follow the example of Christ' (1 Cor. 11:1). It sounds big-headed, but he knew perfectly well that it would happen anyway. He had to be like Christ because it was the truth of his life that the Corinthians would learn whether he wanted them to or not! He commended the Thessalonians: 'You know how we lived among you for your sake. You became imitators of us and of the Lord; in spite of severe suffering, you welcomed the message with the joy given by the Holy Spirit. And so you became a model to all the believers in Macedonia and Achaia' (1 Thes. 1:5–7). The writer to the Hebrews told his readers that they should imitate the faith of their leaders (Heb. 13:7). Peter told church leaders that they must set an example to their flock (1 Pet. 5:3).

A clear-cut distinction between evangelising and discipling cannot be made in the epistles either. The gospel 'came' to the Colossians when they 'learned it from Epaphras' (Col. 1:5–7). The gospel is not just proclaimed or preached. It is also learnt and taught. For the Ephesians to 'come to know Christ' was for them both to hear about him and to be taught in him (Eph. 4:20–21).

In the West we usually think of 'truth' as a philosophical concept. But the Bible does not see it in this way. When Pilate asked his famous question, 'What is truth?' Jesus had already provided his disciples with the answer: 'I am the way and the truth and the life' (Jn. 14:6). Jesus Christ is the person against whom truth is measured. Truth in the Bible is first and foremost a quality of persons. It applies to propositions too, but that is secondary.[2] So the communication of truth is from one whole person to another whole person. It will be less than the whole truth if the process involves less than the whole person.

This passionate concern to pass the faith to the next generation runs right through the Bible. It is linked to a concern to find the most powerful ways to do it, and to commit the whole of life to the task. These are important principles for youth ministry. How does the work of our churches match up? Does it fit in with these biblical principles, or does it owe more to the 'classroom' model of western education? The very term

'Sunday school' often gives the game away. We need to get back to the Bible and to look with fresh eyes at what it is teaching us. Even the insights of modern educational psychology are less valuable for building an effective bridge across the generation gap than the insights of the Old and New Testaments. There we discover that we must encourage questioning, we must stress direct experience, we must build on the lived moment, and we must ensure that faith is experienced as a life commitment by living models.

The basic method of evangelism

How can we apply these biblical principles of communication to youth work? How do our normal approaches to evangelism match up to them?

The foundation of evangelism is a long-term, personal, deep commitment of an individual Christian to an individual non-Christian. The important pioneer work carried out by Oxford Youth Works a few years ago is one of a number of examples where youth workers have given priority to relationships in their evangelism so that the faith can be communicated on this basis.

'As Christian adults we need to seek to form friendships based upon mutual respect. These friendships will take some time to form and they must not be a flash in the pan.'[3]

Just as Jesus called his disciples individually and committed himself to them individually, so there is no short cut available to us to reach lots of people quickly. We can't and we won't.

The Acts of the Apostles and the history of Christianity do record occasions when large numbers have responded at one time to the gospel, but these do not seem to be the norm. The story of Paul's missionary journeys is not a story of spectacular numbers responding keenly to his message. More often a handful accepted, the majority were indifferent, and a significant number were sharply antagonistic.

When he wrote his second letter to Timothy (probably his last letter), Paul looked back on his ministry with mixed feelings: 'You know that everyone in the province of Asia has deserted me,' he wrote (2 Tim. 1:15). It must have been particularly bitter, since Luke records that a few years before, during Paul's two-and-a-half year stay in Ephesus, '. . . all the Jews and Greeks who lived in the province of Asia heard the word of the Lord' (Acts 19:10), and many had believed. Now 'everyone in the province of Asia' had turned away from him. A great awakening had been followed by a is great defection. We like to skim over such passages, as we prefer to view the growth of the New Testament church through rose-tinted spectacles.

On the surface of history there have been great successes and great reverses. But over the centuries, the community of believers has grown steadily and invisibly throughout the world. That is God's work. Our commitment is not to success, however that may be measured, but to do what God commands us to do faithfully. In his son he has given us a clear pattern to follow.

So youth evangelism does not consist of spraying the gospel from some kind of spiritual hosepipe over an open youth club, or inserting an awkward and incongruous 'God slot' into the middle of it, or hoping that the presence of one or two Christian workers will somehow infect a large group of non-Christian young people with whom they are in contact. Nor does it consist just in 'being Christ' to the young people of your town, as you 'waste time' with them outside the local shopping centre.

We are not saying that these are foolhardy activities and that God will not bless them, and sometimes use them to convert young people. He does. But they do not match the model he has himself provided for us.

Much Christian energy has been spent on models of evangelism that derive ultimately from secular rather than biblical thinking, and many Christian tears have been shed over the poverty of the results. Of course, we need to listen to what sociologists, psychologists and statisticians can teach us about reaching unchurched people groups in our society. But God has already shown us the way he would have us reach them. It was the way he went himself when he became flesh and dwelt among us.

This was not a strategy or a structure or a programme. It was a personal, individual commitment. Although what Jesus achieved on the cross was universal and eternal in its significance, in becoming a man he actually restricted his direct influence to a few people in one particular place at one particular time. But from that limited, historical incarnation have sprung the redeemed people of God, as the message of salvation has been passed from one individual to another right down to today. With the presence of Jesus' Spirit in each of his followers, his influence today is wider than it has ever been.

As God became a man to communicate with men, so the most effective communication is from equal to equal. Many adult Christian youth workers see themselves as youth evangelists. God certainly gives special gifts of youth evangelism to certain people, but the most effective communicators of the gospel to young people will always be other young people.

Young people need to discover faith in a concrete way, and the most concrete way is in the life of another young person whom they know well. Adult models of faith are important, but the most immediate impact will be the faith of another young person or, better still, the faith of a group of young people. We therefore need to be setting up opportunities for a positive Christian peer group to be established, so that the faith can be modelled from Christian young people to one another and to their non-Christian peers.

What we are saying here, both about communication and about evangelism, is well illustrated by a common feature of much Christian youth work: frequently the leaders of Christian youth fellowships are disappointed when they arrange an outreach event and ask the Christian young people to bring their non-Christian friends to it. The number of non-Christians who turn up on the night is very few. The young Christians understand the message that they are meant to bring their friends. They agree with it. But they find it very hard to do in practice.

One reason for this may be that the young people do not see the youth leaders bringing their own adult non-Christian friends to adult outreach events. We cannot teach evangelism without modelling evangelism. If we are asking our young people to invite their peers, they must see us inviting our peers. Many youth workers make the mistake of thinking that, because they are involved in youth work, that youth work is their entire evangelistic work for Christ. How many of us have given up trying to witness to our friends and neighbours for Christ because we are concentrating on our Christian work with teenagers? It is far easier to chat about Jesus to a teenager in a youth club than to raise the same subject with our neighbour.

Churches can make the same mistake. When faced with the problem of their lack of impact on a particular part of their catchment area (perhaps a deprived council estate, for example), they come up with the solution of opening a youth club there. While that is in itself an excellent thing, it is not an acceptable evangelistic strategy to solve the problem. The Bible supplies us with surprisingly little warrant for evangelising other people's children. The adults in the church have a responsibility to reach out to the adults on the estate. They should not be allowed to evade that responsibility by passing the evangelistic buck to a couple of their workers who are given a mandate to take the gospel to the teenagers on the estate by opening a youth club.

Evangelism is not some special activity that adults 'do' to young people, like changing a nappy is something you do to a baby, or changing the oil is something you do to a car. It is the natural – and inevitable – fruit of a healthy Christian life. It will be part of all our contacts with other people. Once it stops being normal, and starts being a special activity that we confine to our youth work, we are not only stunting our own spiritual lives, we are also disabling our youth work because we cannot teach effectively what we are not doing ourselves.

A main qualification for Christian youth work should be an individual's desire and ability to share the gospel with their own equals. It seems extraordinary that we commission people for all forms of missionary service without first making sure that they have shown themselves capable of helping one of their own friends become a Christian. The deep, individual, long-term, personal commitment that this demands should be the foundational requirement for full-time Christian service. So much of the Christian church is weak in its impact on society because we have allowed evangelism to become a specialist, results-orientated activity, and not the calling of every Christian to commit his or her life, in depth, over many years, to a few others, in order to help them find Jesus Christ.

We think that we can equip people to communicate the gospel across barriers of age, race, class and culture, when they have not yet communicated Jesus to even one of their own close friends. We think that we can change the structure of our society and the social injustices of our world, when we are not actually managing to convert the individuals who make up that society. We need to regain this vision that the task of winning our world for God is a low-profile, unsensational, long-term task involving you and me. We are the primary evangelists; the Billy Grahams, J. Johns and Rico Tices are not. God has equipped them with tremendous gifts of communication and evangelism in order to give them to us as evangelistic tools for *our* ministry.

It is this model of evangelism that will show us the way to cross the barriers that divide our society and our world. It is the one-to-one commitment of the individual Christian to the individual non-Christian that provides a bridge that can span the gap created by social, cultural, educational and ethnic differences. It is very difficult to relate to a group of people from an entirely different background from yourself, but faced with one or two individuals the task becomes manageable. In fact, after a time you become less and less aware that there is even a problem, as the individuals become more and more important to you and you are more and more familiar to them.

When Mark was working with West Indian and mixed-race teenagers in Balham, South London, it was not the large cultural differences between their various backgrounds that they saw. They saw one another: Mark, Jimmy, Kelvin, JB, Simon, Demetrious, Marc, Martin. They met as friends (and they still do from time to time), establishing and building relationships. When Jimmy (with a mum from Guyana and a dad from Nigeria) sat down regularly with Mark (the son of a retired British army colonel) to study the Bible together, the gap between their contrasting backgrounds faded into insignificance.

This gap will not be spanned by policies and strategies and church committees. It can only be crossed by individuals opening their lives to individuals. David Day and Philip May make the point:

> First, teenagers want people who will share with them. This is often best done in a home setting. They want people to welcome them to their homes and provide them with friendship. This is true of them all, but may be especially needful for teenagers from deprived backgrounds.[4]

We need to be cautious about projects and initiatives that analyse statistics and make recommendations about the evangelisation of our society. We need to beware particularly of those telling the church about evangelism who are not themselves evangelising.

This is particularly a lesson for the youth worker. How can we communicate about evangelism? By doing it ourselves. Our evangelistic zeal must express itself in the commitment of our lives to some people of our own age, as well as to the young people we work with. We must be an example of what we are trying to teach. Otherwise the next generation will be as bad at telling other people about Jesus as so many of us are.

Concrete communication

At this point we are going to look once again at the wider issue of communication. The way Jesus communicated with his disciples has been helpfully described in four stages:

1. I tell: you listen.
2. I do: you watch.
3. You do: I watch.
4. You do and report back to me.

It begins with telling. We start with a message in words. There is no other place to start. If we try to start at another point, our communication will be confused. We worship and proclaim a God who speaks and who has spoken in history. We have no option but to be faithful to his words!

But his words determine not only our message, but also the methods we employ to communicate this message. Paul clearly believed that the message he preached must control the methods he used to proclaim it (2 Cor. 4:1–5).

All too often, however, the communication of the Christian faith confines itself to the spoken word: we told them and they listened. They listened so nicely that, having finished telling them, we told them some more; and, as they listened very nicely to that too, we told them even more afterwards. So we get stuck into *monologue mode,* thinking that it is the best way to communicate, when we have never tried anything else to see if there is a better way.

We cannot communicate the Christian faith as though it were just an academic subject at school. It is not that we do not need to learn it as thoroughly as we learn maths or history. We need to learn it much more thoroughly. And so we need all the insights that modern education can bring us.

Christianity should stretch our minds and require mental effort from us. We devalue the God we worship when we give him less intellectual energy than we give to subjects at school or college, or career exams. Yet that is often what happens. Christian students apply themselves to their academic studies, but when it comes to Christian reading, they never get beyond trivial and lightweight biography. Christianity should challenge the intellect. But it must also challenge the will. It must make its impact on the emotions. It must be related to attitudes and abilities. It must lead to decision and to obedience.

Jesus had a Hebrew idea of learning. This meant that what went on in the mind was inseparably linked to what went on in the body and its surroundings. Integration of the human being meant that education addressed the whole person.

In the western world we have moved away from this Hebrew idea of learning. We have adopted a Greek view which separates what goes on in the mind from what goes on in the body and its surroundings. Our educational system makes us think in terms of the classroom as the location for learning, and the lesson as the method of presentation. We have become intellectuals and academics. We have moved a long way from the 'experiential' methods Jesus used. As John Westerhoff comments, 'We have mistaken intellectual beliefs for faith, and teaching (the school-instruction model) for education.'

Sometimes it is those who are most committed to the faithful presentation of the message which Jesus taught, who are least aware that their style of teaching is utterly different from his.

A study of the way Jesus taught the disciples in Luke chapters 5 to 9 will provide the model for our own work with young people today. There we see the primacy of teaching. The spoken word, whether to the crowds or to an individual, provides the basis for learning experiences. These experiences involve Jesus' actions and the disciples' actions (Lk. 9:1–6).

It is actually stage three of the four stages that is least evident in the gospels' record of Jesus' practice, but stage four is quite clear (Lk. 9:10). If you read on into the Acts of the Apostles, you will discover stage five: 'You tell: someone else listens', and stage six: 'You do: someone else watches', and so it has gone on down the ages until we ourselves came to believe and to be taught the faith. And so it will continue as we pass it on to others.

Our method of communicating the faith must be built on this biblical pattern rather than on a classroom model. Faith cannot just be taught like a foreign language at school. It is to be taught in the way a child learns his own language during the ordinary processes of living. Only in this way can the all-encompassing scope of the faith be grasped. It is seen to relate to everything in life.

Most of us know our own language very much better than we know a language which we learned at school, but the process of learning our own native language was not particularly irksome or painful. Learning French may have been a struggle for us at school. English came a lot more naturally. And we are a lot better at English now. It is the same with the Christian faith. We need to teach it, but we must also find ways of allowing it to be 'absorbed' in the same way that we learned English as we grew up.

We are communicating a way of life. Jim Burns states: 'The most effective teaching that takes place is usually not in the formal teaching times, but rather when the students get to know their youth worker and imitate some of his or her actions. Imitation is perhaps the greatest gift someone can give you.'[5]

So when we lead a youth group Bible study in our front room on how a Christian should not be conformed to this world, a single glance at the surroundings will be enough to confirm or destroy the lessons of Romans 12:2 ('Do not conform any longer to the pattern of this world, but be transformed by the renewing of your mind . . .'). Our living rooms are powerful and concrete messages about how a Christian is (or is not) conformed to this world. And our reaction when they spill coffee on the chairs and tread mud into the carpet speaks volumes.

The following week we might be looking at Romans 13 and a Christian's obedience to authority, but the drive home in the car afterwards will again authenticate or destroy in concrete terms the message of the Bible study. Does our driving show real respect for authority?

If this is the way that faith must be communicated, what does it mean for youth work?

RESPONSE

1. What does your church do to communicate faith to the next generation? Make a list of all the things that you do. If you have a team of leaders, do this as a brainstorm exercise. Try to rank the

things that you do in order of importance. What else could you do? Are there other things that you could do as a church that you are not doing at the moment, which are more important than some of the things that you are doing at the moment? Note down what you need to do in order to make changes.

2. How does your church's youth work fit in with the life-to-life model of communication presented here? Make a list of the opportunities which your young people have to see how the Christian faith is worked out in the lives of their leaders. How could these opportunities be increased? If you have a team of leaders, first write down your answers, and then discuss what you have come up with.
3. Make a note of two friends, of your own age, who are not Christians and whom you are committed to pray for, in order to share your faith with them.

Take time now to pray for them.

Notes

1 *Youth Ministry – its Renewal in the Local Church,* Lawrence O. Richards, Zondervan, 1972
2 See *Knowing God,* J.I. Packer, Hodder & Stoughton, 1973, p 124
3 *Youth Culture and the Gospel,* Pete Ward, Marshall Pickering, 1992
4 *Teenage Beliefs,* David Day and Philip May, Lion, 1991
5 *The Youth Builder,* Jim Burns, Harvest House, 1988

4. It's People, People, People

Working with young people (ii)

If the communication of the Christian faith, both to the believing and to the non-believing young person, is such a total process involving the whole life of the communicator, then there are four important consequences.

The limitations of the printed word

It will make us aware of the limitations of the printed word as a medium for communication. John Benington has written: 'The extent of the modern young person's aversion to the printed word and his preference for the more direct, visual and sensory channels of communication have still not been sufficiently realised.'[1] Many youth leaders and even some young people have been given an academic and intellectual diet which makes them not only accustomed to, but delighted with, the use of the written word. But the majority of young people have not entered that culture, and many of them never will.

Technology such as mobile phones, DVDs, ipods, PSPs and digital television envelopes us in a total barrage of sound, light and visual image, with which the young are now more at home than they are with the printed page. There are far more DVD rental shops in the UK than there are bookshops, and the young person's ideal evening is far more likely to be one of settling down in front of a good (or even a bad) film, than one of settling down with a good book.

Young people are becoming dependent on this new technology. Whether it is travelling in the car with a DVD console in the back of the head rests in front, or the sharp increase of mobile phones amongst young people, technology now saturates the lives of young people. How many of us have had youth meetings or Bible studies disrupted by young people receiving a phone call or text message?

We still have a verbal message to communicate – we cannot escape that – but there are strict limits to the effectiveness of the printed page to communicate it. In the west we have stressed the need for the Christian to have a 'quiet time'. This time of personal Bible reading and prayer, based on the printed page as a method of communication, has proved a valuable and beneficial discipline, although sadly in recent years this discipline seems to have slipped from the lives of many of our teenagers, and also from the lives of their leaders. Maybe that is a further sign that we need to be investigating and investing in alternative means of communicating the verbal message.

But for fifteen centuries the Christian faith spread throughout the world before the invention of the printing press made personal Bible reading a possibility for large numbers of Christians.

It is possible to be a Christian without being able to read. We must not develop patterns of spirituality which deny that. But, having become a Christian, it is likely that a young person will want to develop and improve reading skills in order to satisfy the hunger for God's word which the Spirit has put into his heart.

It is certainly important to prevent one implied message behind so many youth group programmes: that God really prefers those who can read the Bible aloud fluently. We must de-emphasise academic ability as a value within the group. Too many of our young people are being made to feel below average, if not actually dumb, by their school experience. It is vital for them to learn that God does not view them in that way.

The message about God's love for people comes in words, revealed in the Bible, but we have to express it in such a way that even those who prefer a life of emotion and experience rather than thought can begin to think about it, to grapple with it, and to respond to it.

Priority to contact situations

We need to look for every opportunity for the young non-Christian to live his or her life alongside the Christian, and for the new Christian to live alongside the older Christian. It is not more meetings that are needed, but more informal opportunities for the faith to flow from one life to another. We live ever more hectic, pressurised, individual lives, but God calls us out of our individual isolation into a community of faith where he can be silently and invisibly at work between one life and another. So we will have to find ways to open up our lives to the young people we are working with. Two hours after church on a Sunday night with a dozen teenagers and an hour's preparation at another point in the week are not adequate youth ministry.

Jesus spent most of his time with his disciples, whether it was leisure time, routine living, or work. Jesus made plans for his disciples. He monitored their development and had visions for their future ministry. He spent hours in prayer for them. He challenged them. He gave them jobs to do, pushing them out into more activity and responsibility, giving them the freedom to fail. When he was doing things, he took his disciples with him, so that they could learn by watching him in action. He allowed them to see him weak and troubled. (In fact, he seemed particularly concerned that they should witness one of his greatest moments of suffering when he woke the three disciples in Gethsemane. See Mt. 26:36–46.) He continued even to attend to them as he was dying on the cross.

We know that there was a uniqueness about the ministry of Jesus, but all too often we are keen that our young people should see only our strengths. We want a 'pedestal' ministry, where they look up to us as great youth leaders: strong, in control, unflappable, funny, good-looking, intelligent, popular, upbeat, with street cred. So, perhaps subconsciously, we engineer the youth programme so that we do things that put us in a good light, and which play down our own insecurities. 'We never go ice skating, because I can't.' 'I never take our group swimming; it would be just too embarrassing.'

We want our youth programmes to run without a hitch, so that word gets around that this is the youth group to come to – everyone has fun, everyone laughs, it's brilliant, fast-moving, exciting.

Jesus, however, ensured that his disciples saw him weak and in pain. In fact, he went out of his way to make sure that this happened. We forget that God's power is revealed in weakness. When our young people see us weak and fallible, making fools of ourselves, with our brittle dignity shattered, they may feel closer to us and love us more than at any previous time in the relationship. We need to learn to abandon our dignity and our fear of failure. It is when they see us fail and suffer that the model we are providing for them becomes real. They need to see us demonstrate appropriate ways to express anger and pain and grief, as the disciples saw Jesus do.

We should certainly try to run excellent youth programmes, but we must also allow young people far enough into our lives to see us as we really are. 'Techniques in communication can never replace relationships formed out of hours spent together.'[2]

There is a great need for honesty. Young people need honest answers to their questions. They need to find integrity in the lives of Christian adults. It is very easy for a degree of hypocrisy to appear in the life of the youth leader, as we encourage our young people to pray more, to be more humble, to read their Bibles more regularly, but do not practise those things ourselves.

So we must give priority to developing contact situations. We must maximise the opportunity to do things together. Most of us cannot fit many more engagements into our week, so we need to look at the life we are already living for opportunities to share it with others. Teenagers show great interest in the lives of adults – their eagerness to spend time in a youth leader's home; their willingness to help with apparently routine and humdrum tasks, like gardening or decorating; the speed with which they volunteer for any task so long as it is clearly a part of the adult world and not a part of the world of childhood.

At Greenbelt one year Mark asked a West Indian friend whether he would like to come and help him mow the lawn of the cottage where he was staying. As soon as he had asked the question, he thought what an idiot he was. Here was the Greenbelt Arts Festival with a hundred and one brilliant entertainments for the young, and he had asked this guy to come and mow a lawn. Mark tried to backtrack and withdraw the request, but the guy would not take no for an answer. He was determined to come and mow that lawn. It seemed to him an adult thing to do, and therefore preferable to the world of the teenager.

Phil decided to lay a small patio in the back garden, bought the paving slabs, and then had to be away for the day before having a chance to lay the patio. While he was away, one of his youth group did it for him. He managed to lay it in the wrong place, made it the wrong shape, and did not use all the paving slabs, but he was trying to be helpful! And he was trying to come into the adult world.

Such is the aspiration of the young to share in the adult world.

For some of us it may even be possible to share parts of our working lives with the young. It may be worth having 'any driver' insurance cover for the car, so that when we have to take a trip we can ask an older member of the youth fellowship to come as a driver or companion on the journey. What better opportunity for discipling in responsible and courteous driving, and in the use of other people's possessions? (The thought of other people driving our cars is also an interesting challenge to the insidious grip our possessions have over us!)

A young family provides another valuable focus for teenage attention. This is not just a matter of baby-sitting, but of allowing our children to grow up in an extended family where they are cared for and form deep relationships with other young people. Teenagers with personality problems are sometimes relaxed and put at ease by the company of small children.

Marriage and family life must not be put at risk by youth ministry (we will say more about the family, both of the young person and the youth worker, in chapter six), but young people will benefit from seeing the youth leader in his family – praying with his children, asking their forgiveness, making mistakes and apologising to his wife. We do not have to be perfect (or even good) before God can use us as a model. It is the direction in which we are heading that matters – Paul was concerned that people should see Timothy's *progress* (1 Tim. 4:15).

It is important to discover ways to integrate youth ministry into the whole of our adult lives – not struggling to squeeze in yet another evening when we can invite the gang round to our flat for coffee – but looking for the things we are already doing that we can start doing with them. It is possible to take one or more of the youth group shopping at Sainsbury's. You may be amazed that they come (I was at first), but it is an opportunity to take a young person with us into the adult world, and it takes no extra time.

Most of the time in those chapters in Luke (5–9), the disciples were simply 'with' Jesus. He carried on with his ministry of teaching and healing the crowds, but all the time he had an eye on the twelve. It may be right for a youth leader to give up certain things in order to give more time and attention to youth leadership (God means many of us to do rather less, but to do it better). But one dimension of youth leadership is inviting young people to join us in our world, rather than trying to find the time to become like a teenager in their world.

The key to effective Christian youth work is people – people in whose lives Christ is alive, and who will open themselves to young people, not to talk down to them, nor to dominate them with attractive and charismatic personalities, but to show them how to love one another as Christ commanded us. 'Personal work' is fundamental to youth work. We have to build personal friendships. 'Whatever style or approach to youth work we are called to, relationships are always the key to success.'[3] We have to maximise opportunities for life-to-life discipling, where we can live alongside young people and they can absorb the Christian faith from the atmosphere around them.

That is why camps, holidays, ventures and weekends away with the youth club or group provide such a brilliant opportunity in Christian youth work. It may be that the normal pattern of our programme is too dull, too cerebral, too culturally conditioned and too unbiblical in its methods, but time spent away camping, youth hostelling or on a Christian holiday provides a more total spiritual experience. Even if our normal youth group programme is quite outstanding, it cannot match the opportunities for friendship building that a time away together will provide. Take, for example, the female youth leader, away with her youth group: her members see her leading the morning teaching meeting, may have a game of tennis with her before lunch, talk to her about her parents' divorce over lunch, walk down the shops with her in the afternoon, study the Bible and pray with her in the evening, and sleep in the next bed, or the next room, at night. There is a real exposure of life to life. In a weekend's camping most of our pretences have been stripped away by the second morning, particularly if it is raining!

Living closely with someone for two to three days or more is a wonderful opportunity to show them what it is like to be a Christian, and how it works out in practice. We will be able to achieve more in the lives of young people in one weekend away than in many ordinary evenings of teaching meetings.

These activities also have enormous potential for the training of leaders. We have both benefited enormously from being involved as leaders on holiday ventures put on for teenagers. As a new leader works alongside a more experienced leader in such a total form of ministry for twenty-four hours a day, the learning process is fast. You hear about something in theory, and twenty minutes later have the opportunity of putting it into practice. You (should) have quick debriefs after you have done something, and further opportunities to improve as the week progresses. If you want to learn how to be a youth leader, going as a leader on a Christian holiday must be one of the best total learning experiences available.

Getting away from home is another important factor. It represents a step towards adulthood, and it also provides a distancing from the familiar, which allows a greater freedom of thought about attitudes and values.

It also causes certain problems, because residential Christian activities are by their very nature exceptional. They are not a normal experience of the Christian life. There may be problems in relating the more intense spiritual experiences of a camp or holiday to the more ordinary spiritual life back at home. Leaders need to give careful thought to this. It may be wise to play down the emotional intensity of a Christian venture or camp so that it does not contrast too sharply with the life of the youth group at home. The sad spiritual sag in the life of the teenager that can follow a time away from home is a familiar phenomenon, but wise leadership before, during and after the time away can minimise its long-term damage (particularly by developing the links between the home church and the camp).

Young people have a need for adventure in order to change, discover and grow. While physical adventure can meet this need, 'adventure' is not confined to physical activities. The adventure of meeting new people and handling new social situations is even more valuable in a young person's development.

As teenagers grow in maturity, they get less interested in what they are going to do and more interested in whom they are going to be doing it with. The first question a teenager tends to ask when invited to a party is: 'Who is going?' Girls tend to mature faster than boys, and boys remain activity-orientated longer, but older teenagers of both sexes are usually less interested in the activity programme of a camp or weekend away and more interested in its social aspects.

Planning for youth ministry should show a priority to contact situations, because there the communication of faith will be at its strongest. There is a great value in going away together (whether on a do-it-yourself weekend or on a nationally run Christian camp or venture). Youth leaders who have not tried this do not know what they are missing. Youth leaders who have will not need us to say any more.

The value of the peer group

If faith is communicated so effectively from life-to-a-life, then the influence young people exercise upon one another will be enormous. It is extremely difficult for someone under sixteen to hold a set of values different from that of his or her friends. We have noted our need to provide a community of faith as part of our evangelism, so that the young person has immediate and concrete examples of believing to copy.

The Christian life is about change: the transformation of the individual to be like Christ and the change this then produces in his or her social environment.

Change is often painful and frightening. The Christian peer group has to provide a new environment in which change becomes possible for the young person. He is not asked to change alone. He is asked to change together with others. He has examples to copy, and in time he himself becomes an example to others. It involves a process of social interaction. Without this we cannot expect young people to live distinctive Christian lives in a world that is so strongly opposed to Christ. They are called to make a heroic stand against the values of that world, but God provides them with brothers and sisters in Christ to support and encourage them in this revolution.

Christian camps and holidays provide an example of how good teenagers can be at communicating faith to one another. One youth group can have a tremendous ministry to another when they meet up on a residential event. Indeed, spiritual growth in a group, although less spectacular, is often more significant in the long run than spiritual growth in an individual. God deals with each of us as individuals, but he calls us to a communal life as Christians, dependent on one another from the beginning to the end. The normal New Testament word for the Christian is 'saint'. It is mentioned sixty-two times in the Bible. Sixty-one are in the plural, and the only exception is Philippians 4:21 – 'Greet every saint' (although in some modern translations this has been changed to the plural!). We grow in the Christian life together.

Where isolated individual growth occurs it can be vulnerable. When a young person goes away by herself on a Christian activity without a friend or a leader from her home fellowship, the experience may be very exciting, but it is also abnormal. She is not normally away from home, on holiday, on her own, in mainly young company, and in a Christian environment where there are powerful experiences of communal worship and convincing explanations of Christianity. The more abnormal the experience, the less lasting its effect may be. If she has a sense of returning from space travel when she gets home at the end, it is not easy for her to believe that she is still on the same planet. Powerful new resolutions may be made, but a week or ten days is not a long time to work them out. There can follow an equally powerful negative reaction, devastating in its effect on the spiritual life of the young person.

When the same experience is shared by a group of young people who meet together regularly through the rest of the year, it will be less intoxicating. It will not seem so strange and so exciting. But it will probably have a longer-lasting effect on their spiritual lives. What happened on the Christian camp or holiday becomes part, not just of the individual's life, but of the group's life. Such progress was a real part of the development of the whole group. It was probably less sensational because of the continuity with home (there could be less pretence), but it was also more permanent. Opportunities to take young people away together are not to be missed.

We are ministering to groups as well as to individuals. It may be possible to set up small support groups of four or five young people within a larger fellowship. These groups are committed to one another in depth – particularly to support and motivate each other for evangelism. If they are to be effective, there must be a serious resolve not to disengage from one another for a given period.

At this level there can be a much deeper sharing of personal problems and joys. One leader working in depth with four or five young people who meet together regularly, in addition to a larger, weekly, fellowship meeting, is a pattern that has proved very useful in Christian youth work.

The problem of cliques

There is a frequent misunderstanding among youth leaders about the relationship between fellowship and evangelism: 'They are just an inward-looking clique.' 'They are too committed to one another and they will not look outside themselves at all.' 'They don't want any outsiders to come in and disturb their cosy, comfortable, little fellowship.' 'I don't know how to get them involved in outreach.' So says the frustrated youth leader.

But it is probably not possible for any Christian group to be *too* committed to one another. Where there are cliques, the group will often be insecure, with a good deal of concealed jealousy, rivalry and perhaps sexual competition. They are always watching who is going out with whom, and the relationships are exclusive and competitive. The boys compete with one another for the greatest share of the limelight. The group has turned in on itself and is unable to reach out to others, because of a lack of trust between its members.

Where a group of Christian young people really commit themselves to one another in love, they will start to care for one another and to share in a supernatural way. They will weep together when the parents of one of their number start divorce proceedings, and rejoice together when another gets a place at college or a job. That sort of group is characterised by a lack of sexual competitiveness and jealousy. It is able to welcome the outsider because it is secure in its internal relationships.

'By this all men will know that you are my disciples' said Jesus, 'if you love one another' (Jn. 13:35). Not love for the world, note, but love for one another. It is our love for one another that is one of our greatest evangelistic weapons. When a young person experiences a group of his or her friends who have an open, welcoming and supportive attitude, it contrasts sharply with other groups at school or in the neighbourhood.

The test is whether the group contains the sort of socially inept oddballs who are expelled by those other groups (because they will not tolerate the odd, the strange, the difficult and the unpopular as members). Christian groups must not only accept such social outcasts; they must love and care for them. When a non-Christian sees this happen, he is convicted that he has encountered the supernatural, because he knows all too well what sort of treatment such people receive from everyone else.

Evangelism is usually a gradual attraction into a community of faith – that is, into a group of Christian young people who are thoroughly committed to one another. In youth work the main evangelists will be the young people themselves. The major task for the youth leader will be to equip and enable a group of Christian young people naturally to attract others to themselves. The quality of the relationships within the group will be vital to this – we may need to teach them to become far more deeply committed to one another. All too often we think we are the evangelists, and we impose our own evangelistic strategy on our young people.

There is much talk about involvement and participation in youth work. But what are we asking young people to get involved in? Is it in planning and servicing the programme, or is it in ministry to people? Too often we try to involve young people in all the wrong aspects of our youth work: planning programmes, setting up meetings, sitting on committees, and a whole range of administrative chores.

The focus of their involvement ought to be primarily on people – discipling and evangelising. We may sometimes need to take back from them certain responsibilities which should not have been delegated in the first place (like planning the programme perhaps) and start leading them into a people-orientated ministry where they have a communication function, rather than an organisational function. We should make them responsible for people, rather than for programmes.

It is not wrong for them to participate in the organisational aspects of youth work, like sitting on committees and taking decisions, and certainly many decisions about the youth group should be taken after some consultation with the young people themselves. But it is wrong for them to get the impression that this is what Christian ministry consists of. Christian ministry is about people. We want to teach them people skills – how to lead their friends to Christ, how to care for each other spiritually, how to become servant leaders in laying down their lives for one another. The adult leader has the responsibility of doing the more boring 'back-room' work of servicing the organisation, so that the young people can concentrate on the real work of ministry and leadership.

Sometimes the failure of our youth evangelism is related to the inadequacy of our nurture programme. We are not setting an example ourselves of how to reach people of our own age with the gospel. We are not equipping the young people themselves to attract outsiders into their Christian grouping. And when we do encourage them to get involved in the work of the youth group, we invite them to help us with the programme, but not with the people. The work of organising the programme is not the real work of the group. The real work is getting involved with people. It is much harder, but it is much more valuable, and much more fulfilling.

We must first teach our young people by example how, having committed their lives to Christ, they can commit their lives to his people – that is, to a few other Christians with whom they learn to share and for whom they learn to care. Having committed their lives to Christ's people, we must teach them (by example again) to commit their lives to Christ's work – that is to one or two non-Christians with whom they determine to share their lives and the gospel. Commitment to Christ, commitment to his people, commitment to his work – that is a helpful threefold aim for our ministry with young people. We are not training them to chair committees, plan programmes or organise meetings; we are training them to convert and transform the world.

The focus of our ministry

If the Christian faith is to be communicated in the life-to-life manner that Jesus used, then we will have to limit our sphere of influence as tightly as he limited his. It is striking how narrowly Jesus focused his ministry.

For a Jew living in the first century, the whole world was divided sharply into two groups: the Jews and the Gentiles. Jesus concentrated his ministry on the Jews. When he encountered Gentiles, he made his priorities clear, even to the point of apparent rudeness in the case of the Syro-Phoenician woman ('. . . it is not right to take the children's bread and toss it to their dogs,' Mk. 7:24–30).

He did not conduct his ministry in the main centres of population where he would have drawn the greatest crowds. He appears to have moved through the countryside and villages, so that the crowds had to come out to him, sometimes to places so remote that he was concerned that the crowds would starve before they could get back to civilisation (Mt. 15:32).

When they came, he told them awkward and puzzling stories, which we call 'parables'. When they heard the parable of the sower (Mk. 4:1–9), some no doubt shrugged their shoulders and went to look for something to eat, but others gathered round and asked what on earth he meant. Jesus said, 'The secret of the kingdom of God has been given to you. But to those on the outside everything is said in parables' (Mk. 4:11). There was a constant sieving process in Jesus' ministry. He sieved out the genuinely interested from the idly curious. He sieved out the earnest seeker from the crowds who just wanted miracles and wonders (Jn. 6:26).

In John 8, Jesus was speaking to Jews in the temple. Halfway through the chapter many started to believe in him (v. 30). So Jesus addressed himself specifically to them (v. 31). But in the verses that follow he appears to alienate them deliberately, until in verse 59 'they picked up stones to stone him, but Jesus hid himself, slipping away from the temple grounds.' Such a passage shakes our preconceptions about Jesus Christ. It reveals his determination to sort out the true believer from the merely interested.

At the end of John 6 this sifting process led to an almost total desertion:

> From this time many of his disciples turned back and no longer followed him.
>
> 'You do not want to leave too, do you?' Jesus asked the Twelve.
>
> Simon Peter answered him, 'Lord, to whom shall we go? You have the words of eternal life.' (verses 66–68)

However, even among those whose discipleship was genuine, Jesus sifted out those with whom he worked in depth. From among the crowds he picked seventy-two to send out in pairs (Lk. 10:1), but he had a prior commitment to the twelve. Within the twelve, he picked the three: Peter, James and John. Even within those three he seems to have singled out Peter for special attention, and John may be referring to himself when he mentions 'the one Jesus loved' (Jn. 20:2). We could almost say there was a deliberate 'favouritism' in the ministry of Jesus. The Son of God, whose power had created the universe, confined his attentions while on earth to just a few people. Undoubtedly he could have influenced more people – many more were eager to come within his orbit – but there was a clear focus to his ministry.

In youth work we would be foolish to neglect Jesus' example. All too often youth leaders are trying to work significantly with all the young people in their care, forgetting that ten years after they have left there will only be one or two lives that will have been deeply influenced by their ministry. This is going to happen whether we like it or not, so youth leaders need to think in these terms. Jesus certainly did. He worked outwards from strength, building up one or two in a small inner group, and then the twelve, and, from that unlikely beginning, founding a church that has spread throughout the world.

Youth leaders who have realised this have had their ministry transformed. We may delude ourselves into thinking that we can have a significant impact on the whole of our group. We cannot. Work deeply, with a few. Applying that principle works wonders.

Business people talk about the 'Pareto principle', that 20 per cent of our work will achieve 80 per cent of our results. There is no particular spiritual wisdom in that, but it is a shrewd observation of how things are in life. We may not be able to alter the fact, but at least we can be aware of it and pray over that 20 per cent. Jesus spent a night in prayer before calling the twelve.

Every day we spend our time and energy on a great many things that will have no significance in eternity, but there are some things which do have eternal value. We may not be able to spend more time on them, but we can probably increase the quality of that time. It would be good to sit down, think out and pray over that 20 per cent.

That may involve us in a sieving process too. Just as Jesus selected those to whom he gave special attention, so we will need to focus our ministry on those whom God especially lays on our heart. God has called us to work alongside him with those in whose lives he is already at work. As we pray, we need to ask God to give us the discernment to recognise those in whom he is already at work, and then move in alongside him. This is essentially a process of focus, rather than of exclusion. Three times the risen Jesus urged Peter to feed his sheep (Jn. 21:15–19). We have a duty to meet spiritual hunger among our young people. If we do not satisfy spiritual hunger, we are neglecting Jesus' clear command to us.

It may not always be easy to recognise spiritual hunger. We will need God's Spirit to help us. A hunger for the things of God may appear in a non-Christian as a willingness to give serious attention to the claims of Christ. In the Christian, it may show itself as a readiness for greater obedience to God's will. We must detect it and find ways to meet it. Sometimes hungry sheep starve, because their shepherds are too busy entertaining goats. In youth ministry, Jesus' call to us is to feed sheep, not to entertain goats.

We have already considered the danger of dividing young people lightly into the 'saved' and the 'unsaved', the 'sheep' and the 'goats', but it is necessary to exercise our judgment humbly and sensitively in youth ministry. We do not believe, in the final resort, that the work is ours. It is God's work. He does it through his Spirit working in the believer, and on the unbeliever. Our task is to perceive what the Spirit is doing and to join ourselves to him. Our ministry must always be in step with the Spirit. Keeping in that relationship may be harder and more humbling than we expected, but God's Spirit is at work, and whatever he does will last for ever (Ecc. 3:14).

When we focus our ministries on a few people, we are trying to find out what it is that God is wanting to do through us. It is humbling to discover it is rather less than we ourselves thought we could do! But we have the example of Jesus Christ. And it is an encouragement to us to realise the effectiveness of this way of working.

Christ's command to us is to go and make disciples of all nations. The question is, how can we do it?

If we want to obey Christ's command, we must follow Christ's example. That is God's way of reaching people. When a youth leader begins to focus his or her ministry, it does not mean that he or she has no concern for the others they are working with. It is a sign of an *increased* concern for them, because that leader is now taking seriously Jesus' own method of reaching people. If we really love people and have a longing to reach them, then we will confine the focus of our attention to a few. Otherwise we rate ourselves above Jesus, and think that we can do what he did not do.

This principle of focusing our ministry highlights the need for corporate (rather than solo) leadership. The normal New Testament pattern of leadership is corporate (Jesus sending the disciples out in twos, Paul and his travelling companions, the references to elders in Acts 20:17, Tit. 1:5, Jas. 5:14, etc). Wherever possible that should be the pattern in youth work today, and it should be a significant and prayerful aim if we are in the less than ideal situation of being in leadership on our own. Where two or more leaders are able to work together, each can focus his or her own ministry, and by prayerful planning, an overview and strategy for the whole group of young people can be maintained as well. It is part of a leader's responsibility to oversee and care for all the group. To do this effectively, she will need to work with other leaders (unless the group is very small) and to focus her own ministry on a few.

Those few will be the ones in whose lives we detect God to be at work. They may already be clearly committed to the Christian faith, or they may not yet be.

It may be possible to build something into our programmes that provides a sieve for genuine spiritual hunger. For example, we might start a small prayer meeting, or something similar, without any of the trappings that attract people for secondary reasons: no coffee, no comfortable surroundings, no social time. We may be surprised at those who turn up for such a meeting, because these meetings can reveal spiritual hunger in unexpected places.

Spiritual hunger can go undetected when cultural barriers conceal it. A young person with reading difficulties is unlikely to show much enthusiasm for the sort of Bible study that puts a great emphasis on the ability to read. Only persistent prayer will allow us to see young people as God sees them, and to understand what he is doing – and what he wants to do – in their lives. Along with prayer, there is the increased wisdom that shared leadership brings. If we can discuss individuals with one, or more other leaders, it will increase the accuracy of our assessment of those individuals. There is much more to say about youth leadership teams, but one great gain of having other leaders alongside us is the increased insight it provides into our ministries and into the young people we are working with.

For the Christian youth leader, to focus ministry and to feed sheep are not popular strategies. They are not the way to a popular and outwardly successful ministry. Even if our aim is to be obedient to Jesus (rather than to be successful), we will be under constant pressure to meet the expressed needs of the majority who clamour for attention. It is our faith in Jesus Christ that assures us that the greatest need of the majority can only be met by our obedience, not only to his command (to make disciples of all nations), but also to the example he set for us (to focus on a few).

Well matured

To work in this way requires great maturity in the youth leader. That is a vital quality for youth leadership, because there is a clear call to maturity throughout the Bible. No leader can impart to young people what she has not begun to acquire for herself.

This 'invitation to wisdom' is not a call to grow up. It is a call to the completeness that only God can bring to a human being, whatever his age. 'Remember your Creator in the days of your youth, before the days of trouble come and the years approach when you will say, "I find no pleasure in them"' (Ecc. 12:1). This passage does not suggest that the wildness of youth must be replaced by the mature spirituality of old age, but rather that youth is a particularly appropriate time to remember the creator before the onset of old age presents so many problems that a person becomes preoccupied with mere survival. The call is not to become old, but to relate to God in an appropriate way for that particular age.

The concept of maturity keeps cropping up in the New Testament. Paul wrote, 'Brothers, stop thinking like children. In regard to evil be infants, but in your thinking be adults' (1 Cor. 14:20). In some senses we are called to leave childhood behind. 'Flee the evil desires of youth,' he wrote to Timothy (2 Tim. 2:22). To the Ephesians Paul explained that Christ had given various gifts to members of the church:

> to prepare God's people for works of service, so that the body of Christ may be built up until we all reach unity in the faith and in the knowledge of the Son of God and become mature, attaining to the whole measure of the fulness of Christ.

> Then we will no longer be infants, tossed back and forth by the waves, and blown here and there by every wind of teaching and by the cunning of craftiness of men in their deceitful scheming. Instead, speaking the truth in love, we will in all things grow up into him who is the Head, that is, Christ. From him the whole body, joined and held together by every supporting ligament, grows and builds itself up in love, as each part does its work. (Eph. 4:12–16)

He used the language of physical development, but he was addressing adults. It was their faith that was to leave childishness and to grow up to full maturity.

Paul's aim was to 'present everyone perfect in Christ' (Col. 1:28). The growth and development of faith brought him great satisfaction (2 Thes. 1:3, 4). The call to maturity implies that everyone's faith should be growing and developing towards 'the whole measure of the fulness of Christ', an ideal that will not be reached in this life.

This maturity involves a constant desire to keep growing, to push on towards a goal which will not be reached until the next life. Paul wrote:

> Not that I have already obtained all this, or have already been made perfect, but I press on to take hold of that for which Christ Jesus took hold of me. Brothers, I do not consider myself yet to have taken hold of it. But one thing I do: Forgetting what is behind and straining towards what is ahead, I press on towards the goal to win the prize for which God has called me heavenwards in Christ Jesus.
>
> All of us who are mature should take such a view of things. (Phil. 3:12–15)

Maturity is not a static, and possibly rather boring, spiritual quality. It is dynamic. It urges us on. It tells us we are safe in the hands of the one who has made us his own, but it stirs up a great longing within us to become more like him.

The writer to the Hebrews made the same call to maturity. He emphasised that this call began with a firm grasp of basic biblical doctrine:

> In fact, though by this time you ought to be teachers, you need someone to teach you the elementary truths of God's word all over again. You need milk, not solid food! Anyone who lives on milk, being still an infant, is not acquainted with the teaching about righteousness. But solid food is for the mature, who by constant use have trained themselves to distinguish good from evil.
>
> Therefore let us leave the elementary teachings about Christ and go onto maturity, not laying again the foundation of repentance from acts that lead to death, and of faith in God.' (Heb. 5:12–6:1)

If we are to call young people to spiritual maturity, we must first lay a foundation; a foundation of the elementary teaching about Jesus – repentance from trying to justify ourselves in God's sight, and justification through faith in God's mercy instead. The 'infants, tossed back and forth by the waves, and blown here and there by every wind of teaching and by the cunning and craftiness of men in their deceitful scheming' whom Paul wrote about (Eph. 4:14), were those who lacked this foundation and so could not go on to maturity.

The mature Christian knows the basic fundamental truths of Christianity and knows that he knows them. He knows what the essentials are and is equipped to detect 'the cunning and craftiness of men' (Eph. 4:14), as well as 'to distinguish good from evil' (Heb. 5:14). In youth work the call to maturity will begin with the teaching of simple basic truths, which alone can provide the foundation on which to build a mature faith. So discussions on current issues in a youth group cannot by themselves lay a basis for mature discipleship. It may be important that we cover them sometime, and the young people may enjoy those sessions, possibly more than others. But if we are to help them to Christian maturity, we must teach Christian truth, and that means teaching Christian doctrine.

The youth leader who wants to lead young people into maturity must build on the right foundation. The ignorance of the Bible among students at school today does not allow us the luxury of teaching theological fashions or our own doctrinal hobbyhorses. We have to teach the basic truths from which a young person can derive a Christian approach to the immediate problems of his or her life. The doctrine of creation and how it applies to work and to unemployment, or to sexual ethics, or to social justice, would be one example. Another might be our concern that young people should understand how they can know that they are saved, rather than in trying to get them excited at the idea of being saved. Secondary issues (which are often the ones that divide Christians from one another most strongly, like healing or styles of corporate worship) will provide no foundation for a mature faith.

The call to maturity will also include the call to suffer. The writer to the Hebrews made it very clear that 'the Lord disciplines those he loves, and he punishes everyone he accepts as a son' (Heb. 12:6, quoting Prov. 3:11–12). He explained this discipline as an experience of suffering like the punishment a father inflicts on his son out of his love for him. God loves people so much that he allows them to suffer, in order that they may become what they could never become without suffering. 'No discipline seems pleasant at the time, but painful. Later on, however, it produces a harvest of righteousness and peace for those who have been trained by it' (Heb. 12:11).

The good youth worker cares for the young people, not with the love that seeks to shield them from the consequences of their mistakes, but with the love that seeks to help them to learn not to make mistakes. They cannot be shielded from suffering and still grow into mature disciples.

All Christian discipleship involves pain. As we call young people to maturity, we must be open with them about this. We may present our youth programmes as fun, exciting, crazy occasions when everyone laughs, but we must not forget to mention that if the club is to be true to Jesus everyone is also going to learn to cry. The cost and privilege of Christian discipleship go hand in hand.

The Bible does not encourage us to idolise the young nor to glorify the old. But it *does* challenge us to develop a concept of maturity. We need to think through the idea of the 'mature sixteen-year-old', fully rounded in her faith, lacking nothing. That would be an ideal. But it will be the ideal towards which we call the real sixteen-year-olds we find ourselves working with. We do not call them to the faith of a twenty-year-old. We call them to a mature faith, appropriate to their own individual age and development, and we need to be clear what that is.

This call to maturity comes to all disciples of Christ, but it has a special application to the young because it must be distinguished from a mere human call to maturity, which calls young people to grow up in their personalities and intellects. The spiritual call to maturity is not a matter of chronological age. Every age can aim at maturity in Christ.

The discipleship to which all Christians are called is not one merely of enthusiasm and excitement. Jesus promised his followers the same reception that he himself had suffered (Heb. 5:8). This prospect is not welcome to a generation which has grown up with greater material affluence and with less parental control than any of its predecessors. Never has life in the west been more comfortable. Quoting Ronald Hutchcraft, our civilisation is 'creating adults who don't know what to do with delay, discomfort, discouragement, and disillusionment'. Perhaps we should remember that Sigmund Freud defined maturity as the 'ability to delay gratification'.

We are called to follow a most uncomfortable saviour. When our young people are presented with a 'Christianity without tears', full of immediacy and excitement, making many emotional demands but few practical demands, with a stress on 'full-surrender' rather than perseverance, we do them and the gospel a fundamental disservice.

Our picture of discipleship must be one of 'Christianity with tears'. It must allow for the fact that suffering is the rule and not the exception in Christian experience. It must include the virtues of endurance and faithfulness, obedience to authority, submission to parents, self-discipline and self-denial, if it is going to be honest to the New Testament and fair to the age in which we live. Jesus himself never glamourised the call to discipleship. When we lay aside appeals to youthful enthusiasm, we may still be surprised at the power that resides in the simple way of the cross.

We must be quite clear about the long-term nature of the Christian life. John Allan has written:

> Young people are fascinated by the idea of permanence, but in their volatile, fluctuating emotional state, they can't make it work; 'Tracy and Jason 2gether 4ever' carved on the side of a school desk is a brave statement of wishful thinking, rather than a sober calculation of the probabilities. When we ask them to give their lives to Jesus, the idea may appeal, but they will find it very difficult to imagine anything as long-term as a whole-life commitment. They need to be able to envisage what they're taking on; which is why the most effective teenage evangelism is not done in emotional appeals at late-night camp epilogues, or after stunning rock concerts, but in the continuing context of a regular group meeting, where the young person has the chance to see Christian commitment at close quarters over a long period, in the person of his group leader![4]

The normal period of contact between a youth leader and a young person is very brief. But discipleship is for life. We need the maturity to let each young person go at his or her own pace, never forcing a crisis that God has not planned. Have you ever noticed how Jesus dealt with almost everyone differently?

While we do our best to respond flexibly and sensitively to each individual we encounter, there must still be clear priorities in our goals for them. We must aim to teach basic Christian truth effectively. How we do it will vary with the individual, but in every case we will strive to create a clear understanding of spiritual truths because that alone has the power to transform behaviour (Rom. 12:2).

We will want to lead everyone to 'hands-on' experience of the Bible, so that, whatever their academic abilities, their minds are fully engaged with it, for it is in the pages of the Bible that our young people will find out about, and meet, God.

In reading these two chapters on the communication of faith, there may be those who have gained the impression that they are geared to a particular type of youth work (a church-based, nurture-group variety). That is not the intention.

If the principles outlined are authentic biblical principles of communication, then they have just as much to say to Christians doing 'open' youth club work and detached work. They may pose some hard questions for those doing such work, but then they also challenge the presuppositions of much church-based youth work as well.

The theology of communication sketched out here frees the street worker from a success-orientated ministry, judged by numbers. It allows him to work in obedience to Christ in the small and obscure ways that the kingdom of God often comes into our world. It also compels him to open his life deeply to a few in order to proclaim Christ to them in word and deed. It forces him to recognise the priority of the gospel message itself, without which his love and his self-sacrifice will be of no lasting significance; and it does not allow him to evade the responsibility of bringing those he is involved with into living contact with a community of faith (see chapter five).

In appealing for maturity among youth leaders, and stressing the need for patience and perseverance, we do not want to obscure for one moment the desperate need for an urgent zeal to see young people converted. We must temper that zeal with wisdom and maturity, but we must certainly not extinguish or dampen it. If we have overstated the sombre side of the case, it is out of an alarm that this note is missing today. Our responsibility is to be biblical not only in our goals, but also in our methods.

RESPONSE

1. If it's true that 20 per cent of your time produces 80 per cent of the results, sit down, work out and pray over the 20 per cent. Which is this 20 per cent? How best could you use this 20 per cent? What would need to change from the way you use this 20 per cent at the moment?
   If you have a team of leaders, have this as a main discussion item at your next leaders' meeting.
2. Think of two or three young people whom you are working with, and who are most likely to thank God for the deep impact you will have had on their lives in ten years' time. Decide now what you could do to enhance the impact that you have. You may decide to ask each of them if they would like to meet with you once a week to look at the Bible together; or you may think at this stage that a more low key approach, building up the friendship, would be a better use of time. Decide, therefore, how you are going to work better with these individuals. (And then plan to do something about this in the next thirty-six hours, or you may never get around to it!)
   This is a private exercise, but if you have a team of leaders, you will need to discuss with the other leaders, so that you do not overlap.
3. Either think about the following questions, or, if you have a team of leaders, ask one of them to jot down some thoughts about what follows,

to form the basis for some serious thinking at the next leaders' meeting. What is the faith appropriate for a mature sixteen-year-old? What, realistically, is the best that you could expect from a spiritually mature sixteen-year-old? How would this spiritual maturity be shown? Repeat the exercise for the other age groups represented among your young people. What specifically could you do at a group level and at an individual level, to encourage your individual group members to grow to Christian maturity for their age?

4. How word-centred is your communication? Think back over the last three teaching sessions. Can you make it less word-centred, and keep it just as Word-centred? How can you de-emphasise academic ability within the group? Discuss these questions at a leaders' meeting, and then work together to prepare a teaching session which would be perfectly accessible to someone who couldn't read. Then do it with your young people, and ask them what they thought of it.

Notes

1 *Culture, Class and Christian Beliefs,* John Benington, Scripture Union, 1973
2 *Outside In,* Mike Breen, Scripture Union, 1993
3 Ibid.
4 *Harvester* magazine, John Allan, 1985

5. The Anachronism of the Century?

Young people and the church

Monumental irrelevance?

'Boring!'

That is the one word that came up time and time again in a video survey of teenagers outside a Midlands school on a frosty morning one November. Most of them did not go to church, and a significant proportion had *never* been to church. But that was the impression that they had, and so they felt that church was not even worth investigating.

Unflattering caricatures of the church abound, and young people absorb these to form their own image of the church. The Church of England probably tops the list for its contribution. But most public images of church life have created an impression of either irrelevant frenzy, or crushing boredom. Hence the teenagers' comments above.

In considering the relationship between young people and the church (in all its shapes and forms), this image of institutional Christianity as either extremely tedious or distinctly weird ('arm-waving fanatics with their eyes closed, crammed into a huge tent') is an inevitable starting point, and one that we can do little to change in the short term. The outward forms of church life can appear very far removed from the everyday concerns of young people. 'There is a very strong feeling that going to church simply isn't a normal expected part of being a healthy, ordinary adolescent.'[1]

But if the Christian community is over-concerned about its image in the eyes of outsiders, it is set on a dangerous course. Christianity has always been a marketing company's nightmare and historically whenever it has acquired a 'popular' image it has put its spiritual vitality at risk. The issue is not image but truth.

A church which has an enormous popular appeal to the young at a superficial level must call for careful examination. If Christianity is true, and if God deals with individuals at various stages in their lives, then we would expect there to be more old people in the church than young: the longer a person lives, the greater the likelihood that he or she will come to a knowledge of the truth. The reverse would be far more worrying. It would suggest that Christian belief is something to be discarded as our wisdom and experience increase. So the common accusation that the churches are mainly filled with the old may actually be one encouraging indication of the truth of the gospel!

The decline in church attendance during the teenage years suggests that there may actually be an artificially high rate of church attendance among children. Congregations have often focused upon children in their neighbourhood as a suitable target for their evangelism with remarkably little attention either to the Bible or to common sense.

While it is comparatively easy to build up a large children's work or 'Sunday school' (although that is an unfortunate term to use, likely to alienate a large number of those who might come), research indicates that 95 per cent of 'Sunday school' children from non-churchgoing families are not involved in the church by the age of fourteen. Large children's Sunday groups are not always an indication of a healthy congregation. Nor, as we have seen, does the Bible identify other people's children as an especially appropriate target for evangelism. They are no more and no less appropriate than their parents. All too often the church has ignored the parents in favour of the children, perhaps because we think children are easier.

It has also been said that the churches have concentrated too much on trying to evangelise other people's children, and too little on helping Christian parents bring up their own children in the discipline and instruction of the Lord. Thankfully the 1994 International Year of the Family helped to throw the focus more onto the family for a time, and since then a number of Christian organisations have been encouraging churches, through training and resource provision, to take families and parenting more seriously (Care for the Family, for example).

This focus on children's evangelism distorts the age-profile of some congregations and produces an apparent failure at the level of the youth work, when so many drop away again. If, however, the drop-off in the teenage years may be due, at least in part, to an overemphasis on children's evangelism followed by poor discipling of children, then the blame for falling numbers of teenagers cannot be laid simply on the youth leaders, or on the church's youth policy. It may be a more deep-seated problem than that.

On the other hand, as we have already suggested, the fact that Christianity is true will tend to swell the other end of the age-profile of the congregation.

There is likely to be a higher proportion of old people. The *Christian England* survey revealed that the ageing population of the country is reflected in an ageing church population.[2] So not only should the church have a significant number of older people; demographics suggest that this number ought to be increasing. That is bound to influence congregations towards caution and conservatism.

It is at this point that we encounter a more serious aspect of young people's disillusionment with the church. It is not only to those on the outside that the Christian community appears irrelevant. It is those who have a degree of commitment and who experience church life from the inside who face a greater problem. Many churches expect their young people to fit into long established patterns of church services, which the young people neither understand, enjoy, nor benefit from.

So some young people feel that their church is irrelevant to them. As a result, they turn to a diet of Spring Harvest, New Wine, Delirious?, Tim Hughes, Easter People and U2 in order to survive. And this opting out makes it even harder for them to work out their relationship with a group of Christian adults who do not share their musical tastes and cannot live at their demanding pace. Some young people – and some older ones too – question the need to establish the relationship at all. They throw doubt onto our traditional concept of what a church is, suggesting that college Christian Unions, or youth groups, or even youth-orientated events like Greenbelt or the Keswick youth programme may in some senses fulfil the biblical role of churches. Others say that church, where you have young people mixing easily with old, rich with poor, black with white, is an ideal, but an unrealistic one, and therefore they do not seriously try to achieve it.

There is good reason for young people's disillusionment with church. We must listen to their criticisms of the Christian community. Why are we so cautious? Why are our services so traditional? Why do we have an introverted obsession with our own administration and buildings? Why are we blind to the crying needs of the world on our doorsteps? Why do we so often resist change? Why are we so apathetic, so uncommitted? These are questions that rightly challenge the adult church. But we will not deal with the real problem of young people and the church until we arrive at a clear picture of what the church is.

Appearances deceive

The New Testament uses the word 'church' in two main senses. There is the universal church, the invisible body of Christ, into which every believer enters at the moment of his or her conversion (1 Cor. 12:13). The word (*ecclesia*) means 'the called', 'the summoned out'. Paul usually links 'church' with 'God' or 'Christ'; so, for example, we find 'the church of God' (1 Cor. 1:2) or 'All the churches of Christ' (Rom. 16:16), and this gives the Greek term its special Christian meaning. The universal church is the people called out by God at his initiative.

With his massive common sense, Martin Luther in 1537 provided a simple definition of the church in this sense: 'Thank God, a child of seven knows what the church is: the holy believers and the lambs who hear their Shepherd's voice.'

The people who make up the church are a building which God is constructing, and which will ultimately be beautiful (Eph. 2:19–22). Each of them is a living stone which is being built into a spiritual house

(1 Pet. 2:4–5). They are organs of one body (Eph. 4; 1 Cor. 12; Rom. 12), members of one household (Eph. 2:19), and children of one Father (Gal. 4:4–7). But, as a building under construction, the universal church is not yet beautiful or symmetrical. God's family does not always show brotherly love, or demonstrate the Father's perfection. There is a tension in the New Testament's teaching between what the church already is and what it is becoming. There is praise and joy at God's achievement in redeeming his people, and also a keen anticipation of further development.[3]

> But you are a chosen people, a royal priesthood, a holy nation, a people belonging to God, that you may declare the praises of him who called you out of darkness into his wonderful light. (1 Pet. 2:9)

> Instead, speaking the truth in love, we will in all things grow up into him who is the Head, that is, Christ. From him the whole body, joined and held together by every supporting ligament, grows and builds itself up in love, as each part does its work. (Eph. 4:15–16)

Even in this universal sense, the church is not yet perfect. Although she is a bride, who already belongs to the bridegroom, she is spoken for and loved by Christ not because she *is* spotless, but in order that she may *become* spotless.

> Christ loved the church and gave himself up for her to make her holy, cleansing her by the washing with water through the word, and to present her to himself as a radiant church, without stain or wrinkle or any other blemish, but holy and blameless. (Eph. 5:25–27)

With the eye of faith we see what the church really is here and now, and what she will become in God's purpose. This is not outwardly visible. What we see now is a less-than-perfect outward image. And every age has had problems with this – it has always been easy to throw mud at the visible church with all its ugly failings and hypocrisies.

However, if our youth work is not firmly based upon this elevated doctrine of the universal church, it is not based upon the Bible.

The church down your street

The New Testament also speaks of the church in a local sense – 'the churches in Galatia', 'the church of God which is in Corinth'. It talks of a church in a particular place. If *the* church is an invisible, spiritual body of all true believers, then *a* church is a local, all-age, all-class, all-type community of such believers.

Wherever two or three Christians gather together in the name of Christ, he is present with them and they are a part of *the* church. But they are not *a* church. Just before Jesus made this promise (Mt. 18:20), he made it clear that two or three believers by themselves do not constitute a church. If we have a dispute with our brother, we are to raise it first with him, then with two or three others, and only after that to 'tell it to the church' (Mt. 18:15–17).

The Acts of the Apostles distinguishes between the parties of gifted Christians who accompanied Paul on his missionary journeys (and who are never described as a 'church'), and the communities of believers in the various towns they visited (which are described as 'churches').

Michael Griffiths has suggested ten distinguishing marks of the local church in the New Testament:

1. *Location*

The word 'church' is usually used in association with a particular town or city, or even a house.

2. *Organisation*

Paul's concern in the pastoral epistles for order in the local church (e.g. Titus 1:5) shows that it was to be organised, although the New Testament does not provide any uniform pattern for that organisation.

3. *Authority*

Paul left Titus in Crete to 'straighten out what was left unfinished and appoint elders in every town, as I directed you' (Titus 1:5). A congregation was to have elders in authority over it. This is a common pattern in the New Testament.

4. *Discipline*

The writer to the Hebrews exhorts his readers to: 'Obey your leaders and submit to their authority. They keep watch over you as men who must give an account' (Heb. 13:17). The leaders were expected to be sentinels and shepherds who would guard the flock from its enemies and care for its well-being. This would involve 'the corrective ministry of admonition to bring individuals to repentance'.

5. *Initiation*

Baptism would be administered in the local congregation (although it does not appear to have been confined to it in Acts).

6. Communion

The Lord's Supper was clearly a regular activity 'when you come together as a church' (1 Cor. 11:18–34).

7. Teaching

When he addressed the elders of the Ephesian church at Miletus on his way to Jerusalem, Paul strongly emphasised his teaching ministry among them:

> I have not hesitated to preach anything that would be helpful to you but have taught you publicly and from house to house. I have declared to both Jews and Greeks that they must turn to God in repentance and have faith in our Lord Jesus . . .
>
> I have not hesitated to proclaim to you the whole will of God . . . for three years I never stopped warning each of you night and day with tears. (Acts 20:20–21, 27, 3l)

8. Spiritual gifts

The exercise of spiritual gifts is spoken of in a strongly congregational setting in the New Testament (Rom. 12; 1 Cor. 12; Eph. 4). The gifts of Christ to his church could be expected and should be exercised in the context of the full congregation, which included 'husbands . . . children . . . slaves . . . masters'.

9. Families

Paul's famous injunction to 'be filled with the Spirit' (Eph. 5:18) comes in a clearly congregational setting: 'Speak to one another with psalms, hymns and spiritual songs' (Eph. 5:19) and leads straight into a passage applying this teaching to the relations between wives, husbands and children. Families are basic to the structure of congregation. 'A group of students or any other youthful peer group cannot properly be a local church in a fully biblical sense until that group includes married couples with children.'

10. Universal in membership

The local church is not meant to be a gathering of the like-minded. It is a summoned-out group. It exists because of God's activity, not man's choice. It must resist the temptation to become self-selecting in its membership. As far as human relationships are concerned, like attracts like, but the church is a supernatural organisation. It is the word of God which calls into existence the people of God. The church must be prepared to be all-inclusive because the gospel makes its appeal to everyone.[4]

There is at least one more biblical mark of the local church, not mentioned by Michael Griffiths, which is the 'all those everywhere' principle of 1 Corinthians 1:2. The New Testament does not envisage rival Christian groups living close to one another and yet not meeting or even knowing each other. As the number of Christians grew in cities like Corinth, with no special buildings, Christians would have had to meet in different homes (hence, perhaps, the 'I follow Apollos' of 1 Cor. 3:4), but they were all expected to come together for the Lord's Supper (1 Cor. 11:18 – 'When you come together as a church').

This is important for youth work because young people can rarely make sense of denominational divisions. They feel a loyalty to other young Christians in their own area and enjoy the chance to meet up with them, whatever their denominational affiliation.

So the church is both the invisible body of Christ and a series of local congregations throughout the world. The local congregations are the natural focus of the Christian community . . . and mix well together to form a church.

It is easy to cope with the idea of a universal body of believers. The problems arise when we face the truth of the local church, and they are problems we cannot avoid. If young people are to join the body of Christ, they have to join a local community of believers. This is a vital issue which needs addressing for the long-term health of the young people, and for the long-term health of the church.

We may need to take a radical look at the church. Or it could be that we need a radical rethink of how we reach unchurched young people. If the methods themselves do not pay sufficient attention to the church, then the methods may need some critical reappraisal. Any form of youth evangelism which does not take the local church seriously needs to be reformed in order to take account of what the Bible teaches about the church.

Robert Webber commented, 'We all have to answer the same question and that is, "What is our relationship with the Church?" Because, like it or not, that's where Jesus is in the world today.' However disagreeable – and disagreeing – local churches may appear they are God's chosen way of working in his world. So it is with these local churches that we must grapple if we are to help young people into and on in their faith.

And note that nothing has been said about buildings. The New Testament gives us no grounds for thinking that Christians met in any special sort of building, let alone in buildings reserved especially for such meetings. Its heritage of consecrated church buildings is a seriously dubious asset to the spiritual life of the Church of England.

Nor does the New Testament provide a clear blueprint for the organisation, or the leadership structure, or the pattern of initiation, or the form of discipline, for the local church. It is clearly possible to have different sorts of church organisation and leadership patterns, and still be thoroughly biblical.

But the local church *should* have the New Testament distinguishing marks, and in particular it must be a mixture. It will always tend to try to become a gathering of the like-minded. This danger is particularly relevant for youth work.

John Stott has written,

> The Church must . . . exhibit its multi-racial, multi-national and multicultural nature. There has been considerable debate in recent years whether a local church could or should ever be culturally homogeneous. A consultation on this issue concluded that no church should ever acquiesce in such a condition: 'All of us are agreed that in many situations a homogeneous unit church can be a legitimate and authentic church. Yet we are also agreed that it can never be complete in itself. Indeed, if it remains in isolation, it cannot reflect the universality and diversity of the body of Christ. Nor can it grow to maturity. Therefore every homogeneous unit church must take active steps to broaden its fellowship in order to demonstrate visibly the Unity and the variety of Christ's Church.'[5]

Churches often show uniformity among their members in terms of social class, or age, or educational attainment, or financial status, or even psychological type. Sometimes this merely reflects the area where the church is, but if all the members of a church are too similar, it suggests that something is wrong.

The church, in both biblical senses, reflects the content of the gospel. If the gospel is for all men and all women of all races, classes, ages and types, then the church must be just as universal in its scope. Each individual local church must work towards that ideal. It must be an example of the barrierless gospel of the New Testament where 'There is neither Jew nor Greek, slave nor free, male nor female, for you are all one in Christ Jesus' (Gal. 3:28). Paul might have added, 'there is neither young nor old'.

Where a generation barrier appears in the life of a church, it must be resisted as strongly as racism or sexism. From time to time 'youth churches' are tried as a way of helping young people to be part of the church. But even the term 'youth church' is a sadly unbiblical contradiction in terms. The idea of 'youth churches' as a permanent expression of the Christian community's life is faintly ridiculous. They could only be a temporary answer to a desperate need.

If we abandon the vision of a church without age barriers, we are discarding a part of the gospel, just as much as if we accept that there should be different churches for different classes, races or skin colours.

We have seen that young people are today's church, and not just tomorrow's, but we must ourselves be convinced about this; we must convince our young people about it; and we must convince the rest of the church about it. The body cannot function as it is meant to if any part is missing. It is the function of each part not primarily to judge or improve the other parts, but to be committed to them in love.

There is a great temptation in youth work to leave the adult congregation behind. They are apparently conservative and hypocritical. They may compromise spiritually, and they may appear worldly. They may be culturally irrelevant and they may love traditional (and therefore boring) patterns of corporate worship. And above all, they are likely to resist change. So it is tempting to ignore them and to concentrate on the teenagers. The church will not adapt itself to meet young people's needs, so we forget the church and create our own structures geared to the young.

But the Bible does not allow us to do that. It reminds us continually of the unity that Christ and his cross bring to human life (Eph. 2:16–22). Within the church, teenagers need adults and adults need teenagers. Unless a local congregation is striving to unite the conservative old and the radical young, it is failing to live up to its calling, and failing to proclaim the gospel of the upside-down kingdom to the world. 'Teenagers . . . need to be assured that diversity is not only acceptable but actually desirable in the Church.'[6]

We must remember, though, that every individual congregation fails. Every church is deficient. It is not possible to have a perfect church here and now. The New Testament is quite clear about that. In fact, if the first-century church had in any sense been perfect, then most of the New Testament after the letter to the Romans would not have been written. What we actually find in the pages of the New Testament is a divided, quarrelling, backsliding church, within which the New Testament writers encourage their readers to struggle to guard the gospel and hold on to the precious truths that bring spiritual life.

New Testament congregations were mixed. Paul's problems did not lie with the persecutions of the Roman authorities. His problems lay within the church, with Judaising and Gnostic influences which were already there and were damaging God's work. There is not a single passage where Paul attacks the secular authorities who imprisoned him. But he does attack certain people within the local congregations, and his accusations can be vehement – 'Watch out for those dogs, those men who do evil, those mutilators of the flesh' (Phil. 3:2; or see 1 Tim. 6:3–5 and other New Testament writers: 2 Pet. 2; 1 Jn. 2:18–26; 2 Jn. 7–11, etc.). In our thinking about the church we must not allow more idealism to creep in than we can find support for in the pages of the New Testament.

Coping with the minister

We need a thoroughly biblical doctrine of the church as the basis for youth work. It must encompass that exalted vision of 'a chosen people, a royal priesthood, a holy nation, a people belonging to God' (1 Pet. 2:9), as well as the realism that sees the local community of believers as it really is – with all its present spots and blemishes – and warns us that membership is going to involve a measure of suffering and self-sacrifice. If the local church of the New Testament is an imperfect church, we should not be surprised to find an imperfect church today. And we must equip our young people to cope with it.

Too many young people grasp one half of this teaching, but not the other. They are encouraged to have a vision of the perfect church in the New Testament, full of power and evangelistic zeal, and they then compare their own experiences of church life with it. And usually their own church comes off worst. Of course it does. The young people are therefore encouraged to see themselves as change-agents within the local congregation. So Pete Ward has written, 'The life, energy and creativity which can transform the Church are readily available. All around us there are groups of young people whose daily lives reflect this fact.'[7]

But we must teach them the whole picture. We must help them to understand that to change the church they must first learn to love it and to belong to it. We must remind them (and ourselves) that commitment begins at the point of disagreement. Commitment to the body of Christ involves commitment to certain things that I may not like and would not personally choose. We do not choose our brothers and sisters in Christ, but we must love them and be committed to them. This is a supernatural experience and it will have a supernatural effect. The world understands our criticisms of the church. It is happy to join in with them. But it cannot understand, and cannot cope with, our love for the church. That is something supernatural (Jn. 13:35).

Loyalty to the church leadership is often a problem for youth leaders, but it is one very good way for them to model to their young people their own commitment to the whole congregation. Loyalty is another quality that begins at the point of disagreement. While we are in agreement with the senior elder, or the pastor, or the minister, or the vicar, we are not being loyal to him. We are simply agreeing with him. We can only begin to show loyalty when we disagree. Young people are particularly sensitive to the unseen feelings that a leadership team gives out. They probably know better than you do how loyal or disloyal you are to the pastor.

Every worker in a local congregation suffers at times from a minister who is a bad manager, inefficient, slow, inept, or just plain foolish. It is how we handle those frustrations, disappointments and disagreements that can make the difference between equipping young people for effective membership of the church or preparing them for a lifetime of complaining about their local church.

We have already discussed the fact that a normal community of believers will probably have a well-developed representation of older people. This will tend to incline a congregation towards traditionalism. We have to help young people realise that a tradition has no existence except in the people who hold it dear. Traditions are people. When we long to overthrow those traditions, we are in danger of trampling on the fellow-believers who cling on to them. Our commitment to those people as fellow members of the body of Christ has to be weighed in the balance against our dislike for their traditions.

There are traditions that directly contradict the commandments of God (see Mk. 7:9) – which we must oppose – but there are also traditions that uphold God's commandments, and ones that are neutral. We have to learn to distinguish between them.

All too often youth leaders pass on to the young people their own irritation with certain aspects of their local church (for example, the style of the church services). So sometimes the dissatisfaction does not begin in the young people themselves, but in the youth leader. We must take care over what we are teaching our young people by implication and by example about the church. If we never make it to the church prayer meeting, and do not bother with the church AGM, what is that teaching our young people about the importance of the church in our life?

We may be convinced that it is the fault of the adult members of the congregation that young people are alienated. We may be infuriated by the blinkered traditionalism of the adults. It may well be right for a youth leader to lobby for all she is worth with the leadership to introduce a change into the life of her church. It is certainly right that she acts as a bridge between the young people and the rest of the church, acting as an ambassador, and representing the interests of each party to the other. But it is almost certainly wrong for her to whip up dissatisfaction among the young people themselves. She has a far more important and a far more valuable truth to teach them: across all those divides of age and culture which split our world, within God's church 'we are all one in Christ Jesus'.

When a youth group begins to grasp the full implications of this great truth, it is very likely to become an effective force for change within the congregation. People naturally find change threatening. Old people are often uncomfortable with the thought of innovations in the life and services of their local church. They may be frightened by the idea of dance or drama in a morning service, or (if they are Anglicans) having to greet one another at the 'peace' in a communion service. They are able to change only as their 'comfort zone' is enlarged to include the new development.

Young people, who invade the life of the local congregation with an open and loving attitude to adults, can in this way expand older people's 'comfort zones' so that they find they can tolerate, and even enjoy, what had previously made them shudder. It is not that they have suddenly been converted to the idea of dance (or whatever) as a medium of worship, but they have come to know and to love the young people who do the dancing, and it becomes acceptable for their sakes.

The authentic New Testament attitude to church services is one of self-sacrifice: the young singing traditional hymns for the sake of the old and the old singing Stuart Townend songs for the sake of the young. That is the body of Christ in action. It is not a case of the cultural tastes of the old and of the young becoming homogeneous. It is a case of each learning to sacrifice themselves for the sake of the other. That is what the local congregation is for; it is an opportunity for me to sacrifice my tastes for the sake of other people. The question is not: 'Do I enjoy singing this song?' but rather, 'Do others enjoy singing it?'And ideally we can progress to the situation where older and younger people in the congregation are asking, 'How can we change the services to suit them (not me) better?'

It is only by teaching the biblical doctrine of the church in all its fullness that we can hope to arrive at this situation. We sell our young people short if we teach them anything less.

The young often have a strong sense of how wrong it is that the different churches are divided from one another, and a strong desire to do what they can to dismantle the barriers between churches. We must teach them to apply that fervour to dismantling the barriers within our own congregation, and to begin with the prejudices and intolerance we find within ourselves.

We all long to see our congregations change, but we must not allow our young people to put changing the church above loving it. It is only those who have learnt to love the church who have the right to correct it.

Scratching where they itch

So far we have applied this Bible teaching about the nature of the church mainly to young people. But if it challenges them to a new and sacrificial attitude to the older members of the local church, it challenges the adults to bite that bullet as well. The late Robert Kennedy said, 'The gap between the generations will never be closed – it must be spanned.' That responsibility sits firmly on the shoulders of the adult congregation.

We need to educate the older church members in how they can encourage young people to take their rightful place in the life of the local church. Once again we must start from the Bible's teaching. For example, we must take seriously Paul's picture of the church as a body. Many are familiar with this picture (see Rom. 12; 1 Cor. 12), and if they were asked to say how the youth work fits into the 'body', they would probably suggest that it is something like a limb – and perhaps a very important limb, like the right leg. But if we think in this way we are losing sight of what the Bible is trying to teach us.

The 'body' is an organic picture of the church, not a structural one. The different limbs and parts of the body are not different social or age groupings within the church (like the Women's Fellowship, the children's Sunday Groups, the Deacons' Meeting and the Men's Breakfast). The different organs are those with different gifts. Consequently the young people are scattered throughout the body, because they will exhibit many of the spiritual gifts (if not all of them), just as the adult members of the congregation do. Some of the church's best musicians, actors, organisers, givers, carers and evangelists may well be among its young people.

So we cannot consign the young people to one particular, narrowly defined, section of the church's life. We cannot treat the youth work as a neatly self-contained unit which, with the right resourcing and servicing, will deliver mature Christian disciples into the adult congregation of the church on their twentieth birthdays.

Young people must be encouraged to take their proper place in the body by adults who know what that place is and are committed to drawing young people into the whole life of their church. Granted that the majority of adults will have been Christians longer than the majority of young people, it is only right that the adults should be expected to have the maturity to make the greater sacrifices, particularly in matters where personal taste plays a large part, like styles of church service.

The Sunday services are probably not the key to integrating young people into the rest of the church. The Sunday services are the very important centre of the church's life, but as far as integration is concerned, they are more of a thermometer than the place for the treatment to be applied. If the young people were to become more integrated into the church's life from Monday to Saturday, and at other times on Sunday, then the style of our services on Sunday would be easier to make agreeable to all, because there will be give and take for the benefit of others. But the starting point for this is *not* the Sunday services.

As adults we must give serious attention to the uninviting image of so many of our congregations for the young. While the public image of the church is relatively unimportant, the initial experience of church life for young people is important. It must scratch where they itch. 'As it was, is now, and ever more shall be' is not an appropriate slogan for the life of the local church, and especially not if we want it to be attractive to young people. We must not give young people the impression that their local congregation is so resistant to change that when Jesus returns the last seven words on everyone's lips will be, 'We never did it this way before!'

The Christian life is about change, and change as we have seen is a community process. Individuals will not find it easy to change themselves within an institution that is highly resistant to change. Church leaders ought at least to dream radical dreams, even if their style of leadership is naturally cautious.[8] The flexibility that can allow the possibility of radical change is a necessary qualification for church leadership. Where it does not exist, young people will have a sense of alienation from the authority structures of a church.

There must also be an engagement with the real problems of society. A church which has not given serious thought to unemployment, to AIDS and to soft and hard drugs, is condemning itself to a degree of irrelevance in the eyes of the young.

Outwardly the church will always attract the ridicule of the world. Public attention will always focus on its scandals, divisions, failings and feuds. That is why we hear so much about the mistakes and weaknesses of church leaders, but so little about the good, week-by-week work in so many local churches. But the young person who joins the church must experience a living community, responding to its environment and making real provision for his or her needs. A part of that provision must be for peer group discipling and nurture.

Back to the youth group

While we have stressed the need for integration between all the age groups in a local church, the different groupings also have a need to meet at times by themselves. This is particularly true of the young people. There is a healthy balance to be struck between all-age activities in the local church and age-specialist activities. We will be looking in chapter seven at how to achieve that balance, and how to correct it when it tips over. At this point we only want to establish the fact that there should be such a balance, and young people's needs will not be met unless there are some activities provided especially for them.

In chapter two we looked at the biblical balance between the corporate and the individual. Our culture encourages us to over-emphasise the individual dimension of youth ministry, persuading us to see young people as emerging individual adults. The Bible corrects this balance, forcing us to communicate a fully-rounded faith with a powerful community dimension to it, which entails membership of a body of believers totally committed to one another and to their shared task in the world, because they are individually committed to the same Lord. So we have to take the peer group seriously, recognising in evangelism and in Christian nurture that 'no man is an island'.

In slowly changing societies, like those of the ancient world, old age is valued more highly than youth. In a rapidly changing society like our own, youth is prized above old age. The Bible teaches the value of both ages: 'The glory of the young men is their strength, grey hair the splendour of the old' (Prov. 20:29). But within church leadership it is appropriate for the younger to give way to the older: 'Young men, in the same way be submissive to those who are older' (1 Pet. 5:5).

As God values every age equally and deals appropriately with each one, so the life of the local church should make provision for the special needs of all the age groupings contained within it.

Small, medium or large?

It is possible to describe the communal Christian life as taking place on three scales: small, medium and large. At a small scale in the New Testament we see Christians meeting in someone's house (Col. 4:15), and these congregations would have gathered together at the medium scale for the Lord's Supper (1 Cor. 11:18). Large-scale gatherings are less evident, but are hinted at in the concepts of the universal and invisible church, and in the worship of heaven (Rev. 7:9). It is said that all Christians need to participate in the life of the church at all three levels.

Small

For many young Christians the small-scale gathering of Christians will be the youth group or youth fellowship within their local church. But there may be situations, perhaps especially in rural areas where the local church life is so weak that even at this level a structure has to be set up across several churches to provide a viable group. Christian youth work may have to be done across several congregations to provide a proper small-scale meeting for young Christians. Without this, for the reasons we have already discussed (in chapters two, three and four), neither discipling nor youth evangelism will be effective. Local church leaders with a concern for the young in their area may need to work together to ensure that this takes place. We will return to this strategy in chapter seven.

Medium

The medium scale is that of the local church. For the strong biblical reasons we discussed earlier in the chapter this is the most important level. The congregation cannot and must not be a peer group. To some extent it is certain to be a deficient and inadequate community, as we are deficient and inadequate human beings. But as the local church is obedient to the gospel it will endeavour to include all ages, all classes, all races and all types. Every believer should be committed to such a community.

It is important that young people are encouraged to grow out of their youth peer group into an all-age group at the right stage. This will be assisted by a gradual exposure to the adult members of the fellowship. Such exposure will occur in the congregation, but it may be more effective if they are also encouraged to join an adult small group (perhaps a home Bible study).

The official ceremonies of admission into adult church membership (such as baptism or confirmation) are often held at too young an age to help the adolescent with this move from the teenage peer group to the adult fellowship. But the move is vital. Every youth leader should want to see his young people grow out of the youth group and into the adult church. He will want to give them every assistance to take the step. Formalised admission into adult church membership will be helpful, but only if it takes place at the right moment in each individual's spiritual development.

Large

Beyond the small and the medium, there is also a need for larger-scale events. There were times in the life of God's people in the Old Testament when they assembled in large numbers. On those occasions the festal shout may have been one feature of their religious life: 'Say among the nations, "The LORD reigns!"' (Ps. 96:10; see also Ps. 89:15 and Rev. 7:9–10). Clearly there were moments in the New Testament as well when large numbers assembled, as on the day of Pentecost – although there is not a lot of evidence that very large gatherings were a regular feature of New Testament church life. Young people particularly appreciate the experience of being part of a large and united group. Such events can play an important part in their spiritual lives. There are, however, certain inherent dangers in such large-scale events.

'If it's big, it's God'

Local churches need the resources, support, advice and shared wisdom available through para-church activity – whether it is through the denomination, inter-denominational societies, publishers, record companies, conventions, congresses, Christian arts festivals, national youth organisations, book shops or whatever – but structures which work on this level are to serve the local church, not to dominate it. They are a supporting infra-structure, not a hierarchical super-structure. The local church is 'where it's at', not the organisation.

But large-scale events for young people can only be organised at a para-church level. So youth organisations have a role to play as servants to the youth work of the local church. They may start fresh initiatives across the country to encourage and assist local youth workers. The youth work of many local churches has benefited enormously from nationally or centrally organised events, but the leadership of the local church must be respected and not imposed upon. Unless we hold to a biblical order of importance in this area, there will be many problems.

We need to be careful too with the maverick Christian worker, who likes to sit loose to the local church and to criticise it, but is careful to have no proper relationship to it. He is therefore not discipled by, nor does he let himself come under the authority of, the local church, and he is a spiritual danger to himself and to others. Sadly, he is not an unfamiliar figure in Christian youth work.

We also need to ask this question: 'Where does God speak to his church?' Does God speak in some special way at an event like Spring Harvest, but not in the local congregation? When a large and powerful organisation decides to hold an event at short notice which overthrows the long-standing plans of a smaller organisation, who is to decide which of them God was actually guiding? If it's big, it does not necessarily mean it is straight from God!

There will be the problem of where pastoral responsibility and authority over young Christians lie. The Bible teaches that we are to submit to those who have responsibility for our souls: 'Obey your leaders and submit to their authority. They keep watch over you as men who must give an account' (Heb. 13:17). Exactly the same idea is specifically applied to young people at the beginning of 1 Peter 5. In other words, the young are to submit to those who work among them and have spiritual responsibility for them, not to superstar preachers and mega-watt-PA-video-wall youth organisations.

It is a mistake for the leadership of a para-church organisation to expect from its teenage members a loyalty which ought to be directed to the local church leaders. The local leaders, on the other hand, should assume full responsibility for their young people, and not, for example, send their members on a holiday venture while not dreaming of going themselves, so at least partially abdicating responsibility for their members' spiritual wellbeing.

And the youth organisations must not look down on local church leadership, seeing themselves as the trend-setters, God's prophetic voice to the youth work of the church. Similarly, local youth leaders must not look up to national organisations, assuming that their size and the up-market nature of their publicity automatically supplies them with the answers to the particular problems of a particular local church situation. The Bible reverses this relationship and teaches us to put the youth work of the local congregation above that of the national youth organisation.

So in all our youth work, we need a constant reminder to do something which it is very easy to forget: *Think local church.*

RESPONSE

1. Consider what you can do to help your young people get to know the older members of the church, and vice versa. Jot down some ideas and discuss them at your next leaders' meeting. Why not try one of these?
   a) Borrow a camcorder and video members of your church after the service one Sunday. Interview some members of the church, and ask them how long they've been coming to the church, what they like most about it? etc.
   b) Photograph some prominent members of the church, and ask your members to put names to the faces. Have a memory test next week. Have a long-term display of the photos in

your group. Do the same with members of your group, and display these for the other members of the church to have a look at, and so get to know members of the youth group.

2. At your next leaders' meeting, brainstorm how your young people could get more involved in non-Sunday activities that your church runs, e.g. plan to visit all the church meetings during the next half-term holiday.
3. If you are thinking of planning a para-church event, perhaps in conjunction with other churches, here is a checklist of questions to work out whether it is the best use of time and resources:
   a) What will this event (or whatever) do for the body of Christ? (i.e. what effect will it have? Not: what is our motive in putting it on?)
   b) Does it fit into the work of the church:
      (i) nationally? (In other words, have we taken into account all other events that might clash or overlap? Remember that similar events two months apart may actually clash in terms of preventing young people with little money going to both of them. Have we consulted all other organisations that have a shared concern in this area?)
      (ii) locally? (In other words, do local youth leaders want it? Does it take into account and assist their work?)
   c) What effect will it have on the expectations and loyalties of the young people involved? Will it help to integrate them

into the worshipping community of local congregations?

d) Will it be sensitive to the emotional vulnerability of teenagers? Or will there be unhelpful pressure to create in the lives of the young people crises that have not been planned by God?

e) In the present situation, is it necessary? (Not 'Will it be successful?')

Notes

1 *Teenage Beliefs,* David Day and Philip May, Lion, 1991
2 The Christian England Survey, MARC Europe, 1989
3 For further reading on this see *God's New Community,* Graham Beynon, IVP, 2006
4 *Cinderella with Amnesia,* Michael Griffiths, IVP, 1975
5 *Issues Facing Christians Today,* John Stott, Marshalls, 1984
6 *Counselling Teenagers,* Keith Olson, Group Books, 1984
7 *Worship and Youth Culture,* Pete Ward, Marshall Pickering, 1993
8 For further reading on this issue see chapter five of *Don't Waste Your Life,* by John Piper, Crossway, 2003. It is an excellent chapter and well worth reading regularly.

6. Going, Going, Gone

Young people in the family and the school

Much of adolescence is spent either at home or at school, so those involved in Christian youth work need an understanding of the Bible's teaching on the family and on education. They play such an important part in the life of a young person that the youth leader must have a clear biblical perspective on them. As there is far more biblical material directly related to the family, we will start here and deal more briefly with the school at the end of the chapter.

God as Father

A Christian understanding of the family is important because God speaks of his relationship to his people most often in terms of a father and his children:

> As a father has compassion on his children,
> so the LORD has compassion on
> those who fear him. (Ps. 103:13)

> My son, do not despise the LORD's
> discipline and do not resent his rebuke,

because the LORD disciplines those he loves,
as a father the son he delights in. (Prov. 3:11–12)

The Lord's Prayer (Mt. 6 and Lk. 11) and the parable of the prodigal son (Lk. 15) develop the idea. Jesus completed it by calling God 'Abba' – 'Dad' (Mk. 14:36), and teaching his followers to do the same through his Spirit (Rom. 8:15–16).

While human fatherhood teaches us something about our heavenly Father, it is more significant that our heavenly Father teaches us much about human fatherhood (and motherhood). Paul wrote, 'For this reason I kneel before the Father, from whom his whole family in heaven and on earth derives its name' (Eph. 3:14–15). Bishop Severian of Gabala commented on this in the fifth century: 'The name of Father did not go up from us, but from above came to us.'

It is sometimes said that to speak of God as a father is unhelpful, because so many people have unhappy experiences of their own human fathers. It is true that family life is under strain today, but the concept of God as a parent – he is also sometimes spoken of in terms of motherhood (Deut. 32:10–12, 18; Is. 66:12–13; Lk. 13:34) – is so central to the Bible's teaching about his revealed character that it cannot be ignored. It may be helpful to talk of God as the *good* Father, recognising that not all human fathers are good, but maintaining the need to understand what fatherhood is about. Let's not throw out the baby with the bathwater, because the idea of God as a father provides powerful guidelines for family life.

Conflict between the generations

Conflict and stress within the family are nothing new. The pace of change in our century has increased our sense of the distance between the generations, but the Bible too is concerned with the problem of the generation gap. There are specific examples of conflict between the generations, like King Rehoboam and his advisers. When he succeeded his father Solomon, Rehoboam was challenged to predict the style in which he would rule (1 Kgs. 12:1–16). He consulted first his father's generation and then his own, and took the latter's advice ('My father scourged you with whips; I will scourge you with scorpions') with disastrous consequences.

We have already considered the Bible's stress on the need for each generation to communicate spiritually with the next generation (chapter three). The Bible also contains many examples of the failure to do so effectively.

Eli's failure with his own sons, Hophni and Phinehas, contrasted with his success in bringing up Samuel as a faithful servant of God (1 Sam. 1–4). (And if Eli and Samuel can be seen as a youth group, here is a salutary warning to youth leaders not to neglect their own children. Our children are more important than our youth group.) But then the same pattern set in with Samuel: 'When Samuel grew old, he appointed his sons as judges for Israel . . . But his sons did not walk in his ways. They turned aside after dishonest gain and accepted bribes and perverted justice' (1 Sam. 8:1–3). David's spiritual stature as a man after God's heart was not communicated effectively to his children if Absalom was anything to go by. Even Solomon fell far short of his father's zeal for God.

Conflict within the family and between the generations is a consequence of the Fall (Cain and Abel, Gen. 4), and is a distinct feature of 'the last days' (2 Tim. 3:1–5). The Old Testament ends with a lovely prophecy of restored harmony between the generations: 'He will turn the hearts of fathers to their children, and the hearts of the children to their fathers' (Mal. 4:6). This prophecy is picked up and applied to the work of John the Baptist when the angel told Zechariah: 'he will go on before the Lord, in the spirit and power of Elijah, to turn the hearts of the fathers to their children and the disobedient to the wisdom of the righteous – to make ready a people prepared for the Lord' (Lk. 1:17).

What the Bible has to teach about family life is realistic and relevant for an age like our own where the family is under attack. It addresses itself to the problem of the generation gap and promises us that it is God's purpose to resolve it (see Prov. 17:6).

There are particular pressures on the family today. There are social trends such as the erosion of the extended family, the rise in the divorce rate, the increase in illegitimate births, the legalisation of civil partnerships, and the rampant materialism of Western society. More than two in three marriages now end in divorce (with 153,399 in 2004),[1] and more and more couples do not see the need to get married in the first place. In the UK, in 2004, 28 percent of British families with children were single parent families. About 25 percent of UK children lived in single parent families. This is three times the percentage in 1972, when just one in seventeen children lived in a single parent family. Another interesting, yet desperately sad, statistic is that over 40 percent of families with childrens in suburbs of London are single parent families, that is double the UK average.[2]

Nevertheless, our society continues to have very high expectations of marriage and of the family. Many people expect marriage to solve their deepest longings for personal fulfilment, while the family home is seen as a place of love and security – 'a do-it-yourself reality kit', which can take the place of a relationship with God in giving human lives meaning.

While marriage and the family are for many their greatest haven, they may also be the greatest stress point. There can be few more stressful experiences than taking your young children to Toys R Us on a Saturday afternoon! Statistically, the most dangerous person in the world is your own spouse. Julia Roberts starred in the film *Sleeping with the Enemy* (1991). And who was 'The Enemy'? Her husband. The Bible makes it clear that family life will be tough. And contemporary writers on parenting agree:

> First, parenting will always be a struggle. Even the godliest parent will have to labour hard to provide unconditional involvement and uncompromising responsiveness for his kids on a consistent basis.[3]

It is in the family that relationships are at their most intense. Samuel Butler commented, 'One of the surest signs of our Lord's extraordinary effect on people was the fact that Simon Peter continued to follow him after he had healed Peter's mother-in-law!'

Order in the family

So the need for ordered relationships in family life is heavily stressed. The Old Testament law spelt out the severest consequences for a son's disobedience to his parents:

> If a man has a stubborn and rebellious son who does not obey his father and mother and will not listen to them when they discipline him, his father and mother shall take hold of him and bring him to the elders at the gate of

> his town. They shall say to the elders, 'This son of ours is stubborn and rebellious. He will not obey us. He is a profligate and a drunkard.' Then all the men of his town shall stone him to death. You must purge the evil from among you. All Israel will hear of it and be afraid. (Deut. 21:18–21)

This punishment, which seems inappropriately severe to our way of thinking, indicates the importance of order in the home. Stoning for being disobedient to your parents does not receive any endorsement in the New Testament, but the importance of children obeying their parents does: 'Children, obey your parents in everything, for this pleases the Lord' (Col. 3:20; cf. Eph. 6:1–3).

There is not a hierarchy in the home in the sense that the older generations are more important or more valuable than the younger ones, but there must be order in the home. A man who does not provide for his own family is worse than an unbeliever (1 Tim. 5:8). When Paul instructs children to obey their parents, he immediately instructs fathers not to provoke or irritate their children lest they become angry and rebel (Eph. 6:4), or become depressed and lose confidence in themselves (Col. 3:21). Within the family there is a 'headship', a leadership in submission, given to the husband: a role which requires greater sacrifice and humility than that demanded of the wife (Eph. 5:21–33).

It is the father's responsibility to see that the relationships within the home are well ordered. When focusing on local church leadership in the pastoral epistles Paul makes this clear: 'He must manage his own family well and see that his children obey him with proper respect. (If anyone does not know how to manage his own family, how can he take care of God's church?)' (1 Tim. 3:4-5; see also verses 12–13).

Paul here sets higher standards for church leaders than could be expected of other believers, as Titus is instructed only to appoint elders whose children are believers. However good a father and a husband a Christian man may be, he cannot guarantee that his children will also believe. But he can take responsibility for the ordering of his home life in obedience to God's will.

The correct order of priority is that the man must first put God in the centre of his own life. He then seeks to run his family according to God's will as revealed in the Bible. He does this primarily for God's sake, out of obedience to him. Adrian Rogers has written, 'I've been a pastor many years, and I have yet to see a home where the wife and children did not follow the man if he, from the beginning of the marriage, loved and served God.'[4] Loving and serving God will mean being the best possible husband and father that a man can be.

Our society places a distorted emphasis on the acquisition of possessions and this puts great pressure on husbands to pursue successful careers. The pursuit of a successful career, even if it does not bring financial rewards, confers status on a man and may provide him with considerable personal gratification. But this 'idolatry of the career' deters husbands from giving to their homes and families the time and energy needed to lead them in the way God requires.

The importance of family life

As we have seen, the home is not an easy place. The trials and tribulations of family life are obvious.

Parenting teenagers today can be scary. The average parent of an adolescent is worried – worried about the child's welfare, moral choices, friends, education, and complexion, not to mention the fungus that's growing on the walls of the teen's bedroom. It's usually while parenting adolescents that we learn what it means to pray unceasingly![5]

The Bible does not encourage us to see it in any other way. The process of 'deparenting', whereby a child gradually becomes independent of his or her parents (a process that starts at birth), is more painful for the parent than for the child. 'The parent must gain his freedom from the child, so that the child can gain his freedom from the parent.'[6]

Just when an adolescent in a family may be facing serious developmental tasks, as she moves out of the home into a peer group, her parents may be facing equally serious developmental tasks in maintaining a certain standard of living, parenting a teenager, developing adult recreational activities, adjusting to their own and their spouse's physiological changes, or coping with ageing parents. A family is a dynamic unit – every member is changing all the time. It is not just the children who develop while the adults are static and stable – fixed anchor points within the relationship. Adults have their own developmental tasks to contend with as well.

The 'problem' of teenage children is sometimes also the 'problem' of parents facing their own mid-life crises. The stress of going through the menopause can arrive at the same time as the stress of having rebellious teenage children – it can be a formidable combination. There is nothing wrong with either the menopause or the teenage years, but those experiencing them have special emotional needs which will make special demands on family life.

Many men and an increasing number of women never channel into their family life even a tiny proportion of the time and energy that they give to their career. And this can be just as true of those in full-time Christian work as those in a secular job. In fact, the more 'elevated' the job or vocation, the more likely it is to cause a man (or woman) to upset God's order for family life. Those in Christian work or in a caring profession (like medicine or social work) are most tempted to put the demands of their work above their calling to be husbands and fathers, or wives and mothers.

We can picture God's order of priorities as a series of concentric rings around an individual. The innermost ring represents his (or her) individual relationship with God, the next the relationship with the spouse, the third is the relationship with the children and with parents. Only after that comes ministry to others. For the single person there may only be a 'parents ring' between the personal relationship with God and wider ministry, which is why single people are so precious to the church – they have a capacity for wider ministry denied to the married.

There is clearly overlap between each ring, but the point is that we cannot and must not ignore these circles. We must approach youth ministry through the rings of our other responsibilities. We cannot jump them. If we try to bypass them, we jeopardise all our activity – our 'ministry' and our family life as well.

We will never get our relationships with our spouses right, until we first get our relationship with God right. We will never get our relationship with our children right, until we first get our relationship with their mother/father right. If we are involved in youth work, we will never pastor young people properly until we first relate properly to our own children and our own parents.

Our ministry can become a god, on the altar of which we sacrifice (perhaps unwittingly at first) our marriage and our children. That is not God's purpose for us, but neither does he want us to confine ourselves exclusively to the central rings. He means us to work out from them into ministry for others.

The Bible does not present the family to us as a haven of security and pleasure, but it does provide us with clear guidance that we should give time and energy to how we conduct our family life. This is not a low priority. It is more important than our careers; it is more important than our standard of living; it is more important than the education of our children; it is more important than our youth work. The pressures that oppose this Christian teaching are threefold:

1. **The myth of the 'happy family'**, still seen on many adverts, creates an unrealistic and harmful notion of domestic bliss, so that we are always chasing an unobtainable ideal. The reality may be more like this: 'Young people in the next decade will know little of trustworthy relationships. Most will be psychological orphans.'[7] Marriage and the family will for many be the place where they experience their greatest happiness: they will also be the place where God teaches us our hardest and most painful lessons.

2. **The quest for material possessions**, which never tires of trying to deceive us that life *does* consist in the abundance of our possessions. It substitutes material values for spiritual ones, so that we start to believe that the houses we live in, the cars we drive, the gadgets we enjoy, the decor we arrange, the possessions we delight in, the holidays we go on, the pets we keep, the toys we provide, will actually make a concrete

contribution to the happiness of our family life. They cannot, and they will not, because happiness lives in a quite different place.

3. The 'idolatry of the career' which persuades us never to question the work ethic of our jobs, so that an offer of promotion amounts to guidance from God. It is not to be questioned on spiritual grounds – the effect it will have on our family life, on our friendships, and on our participation in the life of the church. Why is it so refreshing when we hear of Christians who have turned down promotion because there are more important things in life than working a huge number of hours to earn huge amounts of money which we never have time to enjoy? Perhaps Christians who are on a successful (or potentially successful) career path should consider their attitude to the first commandment: 'You shall have no other gods before me' (Ex. 20:3).

The dangers of determinism

If the Bible stresses the importance of family life and of ordered relationships within the home, it also provides a pattern for parenting. God is a Father whose first son, Adam, chose to disobey him. He did not then press the delete button and rewrite the script. He had made Adam in his own image and had granted him freedom and dignity. Adam expressed that freedom by disobeying his Father and they both suffered the consequences.

As parents, God calls us to be to our children what he is to us. We will not control what we bring into the world. Our children are not our pets, and they are not just an extension of ourselves. They are a temporary trust from God.

Many parents today believe that it is their job to create a desirable character and good habits in their child, and that any shortcoming is their fault. This belief springs from the myth of 'determinism' – the view that every effect is the inevitable result of certain causes – and it removes from the individual the freedom and dignity which God has given to him or her. And it fills parents with guilt.

Experience tells us that good parents do not *always* produce good children and bad parents do not *always* produce bad children. Clearly there are a great many factors involved in the development of a personality. Heredity and environment play their part, but the Christian view of humankind will always assert the God-given freedom and dignity of each individual as well. We are not helpless victims of our genes, our upbringings and our circumstances. We are beings created in the likeness of God with a will of our own, and with the ability to choose. Determinism would steal that from us. Parents should not always feel guilty because their children do not turn out well, nor can they take all the credit when their children do. Parents are important in the upbringing of their children, but there are other factors as well in the equation.

We are not given our children by God so that we can boast of their good points or be ashamed of their failures. John White's basic rule of parenting is 'As God is to me so must I be to my children.'[8] Our aim is to be godly parents, not successful social scientists. We will go astray if the question uppermost in our minds is 'How can I rear my children successfully?' That has only one answer: 'I cannot, because they are not my products.'

However, if the question is: 'How can I be a good parent?' then the answer is: 'As God is.' So we do not try to be good parents for our children's sake, but for God's sake. As Christian fathers, we keep an eye upon our heavenly Father and we try to conduct ourselves according to his will, not according to what we hope the effect will be in the life of our children. We trust that result to God.

The search for personal worth

So we must try to allow our children the freedom and the dignity that God grants to us. Parents allow their children increasing freedom to choose, not because they do not care about them, but rather because they *do* care. They grant them dignity and respect by allowing them an increasing freedom within the order of a Christian home, because God grants dignity and respect to humankind.

The home plays a vital part in building up the self-esteem of a child. God makes it clear that he values every human being highly – not just by creating them in his own image with freedom and dignity, but also by sending his own Son to die for them: 'For you know that it was not with perishable things such as silver or gold that you were redeemed from the empty way of life handed down to you from your forefathers, but with the precious blood of Christ, a lamb without blemish or defect' (1 Pet. 1:18–19). Human parents have the task of instilling personal worth in their children, and this is not a task that can be delegated.

James Dobson has written: 'Personal worth is not something human beings are free to take or leave. We must have it, and when it is unobtainable, everybody suffers.'[9] So, for example, there is often a link between irresponsible sexual behaviour and low self-esteem. Adolescents with the greatest sense of inferiority are those most vulnerable to sexual experimentation and exploitation. 'Lack of self-esteem produces more symptoms of psychiatric disorders than any other factor yet identified.'[10] Our society attaches great value to good looks. We reward the attractive and penalise the ugly from the earliest days of life. Significantly, most of us do not think we are good-looking. Particularly during the growth spurt of puberty, young people are highly conscious of their looks. One study of two thousand teenagers asked the question, 'What do you most dislike about yourself?' Skin problems outranked every other reply by a wide margin.

The other item of great value in our society is ability, particularly intellectual ability. The development of universal education in the West has given academic ability social prominence. For many young people, however, their time at school is one long painful assault on their self-esteem. Parents are naturally concerned to know whether their child is above or below the average of the class. And so, because of the way statistics work, half of the young people in the country are in danger of being labelled 'below average', or even 'slow'. That does not do much for their self-esteem. It is wise to de-emphasise academic achievement as a value in the home (it is not, after all, something that God rates highly), and to help the slow learner to find his compensating skills.

The Bible teaches that family life should be regulated in such a way that each member can discover their own worth and so build up their own confidence: The Living Bible's translation of Ephesians 6:4 is:

> And now a word to you parents. Don't keep on scolding and nagging your children, making them angry and resentful. Rather, bring them up with the loving discipline

the Lord himself approves, with suggestions and godly advice.

The parents' task within the family is to shape the child's will, but also to preserve and strengthen the child's spirit. This task is particularly important during adolescence when the urgent search for identity can create a crisis of self-confidence (although it must start long before then). Teenage suicides and attempted suicides (and psychologists tell us there is a significant difference between the two) point to a crash in self-esteem among some teenagers. Attempted suicides are more common among teenage girls, but teenage boys succeed more often. 'The agony of heart in the fifteen-year-old boy who jumped off Clifton Suspension bridge to his death, following his request for a psychiatric appointment to cure his blushing, can only be guessed at.'[11]

It is God's purpose that there should be ordered relationships within the home in order to allow the young to grow up with a strong sense of their own value.

Learning the lessons for youth ministry

Anyone working with young people needs a Christian understanding of how family life should work. This is, first, because we must get our own family life on sure foundations.

As we saw earlier, Eli was someone who was much better with someone else's child, Samuel, than he was with his own children, Hophni and Phinehas (1 Sam. 1–4). It is a pattern that is all too familiar in Christian youth work, but notice what then happened to Samuel: he himself judged Israel justly, but when his sons, Joel and Abijah, succeeded him as judges in Beer-Sheba, they 'did not walk in his ways'. 'They turned aside after dishonest gain and accepted bribes and perverted justice' (1 Sam. 8:1–3). It was Hophni and Phinehas all over again.

Eli had shown Samuel how to walk uprightly himself, but he had never shown him how to bring up his own sons in the fear of the Lord. He had not provided Samuel with a model of godly parenting. Neither of them as fathers could have forced their sons to be godly, however much they desired it, but they both revealed their weakness and inadequacy as parents by allowing their ungodly sons to succeed them as priests and judges over Israel. Moreover that pattern of weak fatherhood was effectively communicated from Eli to Samuel.

So, a proper understanding of – and obedience to – God's order for the family is a prerequisite for Christian youth work. Two of the best books for the youth worker widely available today are both actually about the family. Neither are new publications (the first one has recently been re-released however), but they are both excellent ones: *The New Hide or Seek* by Dr James Dobson (Revell, 2001) and *Parents in Pain* by John White (IVP, 1979). They contain tremendously useful teaching about youth work and we have drawn heavily on them both in this book.

Much damage can be done in youth ministry by well-meaning people who have not yet worked out God's order of priority in their own lives. We must not sacrifice our families or our marriages for the sake of our ministries. We cannot teach others to obey the fifth commandment ('Honour your father and your mother' – Ex. 20:12), unless we have a proper respect for our parents. We may endeavour to teach the Bible faithfully, but our lives will be contradicting it. What we model with our lives will probably prove more influential in the long run than what we say with our Bible-teaching programmes.

The fatherhood pattern

There is another solid theological reason for grounding youth work in an understanding of parenting. This is that God has provided a pattern for our theological understanding of him by calling himself a Father.

This is the way his relationship with us is most often expressed. It gives us an understanding of why we are permitted the freedom to rebel against him, to spoil our lives and to destroy his creation. It also helps us to grasp the liberty of the children of God: once our relationship with him has been restored through Jesus (when we forsake our rebellion and accept forgiveness because Jesus died in our place to take the consequence of that rebellion), then we start to grow up into 'adult' children.

This not only shows us how we ought to behave as human parents, giving freedom, dignity and self-respect to our children. It also has important lessons for youth ministry. We must grant to young people the same dignity and respect that God accords to all people.

On the one hand, God allows his children to rebel. He does not withdraw their freedom at the moment of disobedience. Although he paid the highest price to obtain our salvation, he never violates the integrity of the person who chooses to turn away from him and to spend eternity apart from him in hell. With infinite sadness he endorses that choice, turning his own eyes away (Hab. 1:13), giving that person up (Rom. 1:24, 26,

28), and forsaking him as he has forsaken God (Mk. 15:34).

One of the hardest experiences in youth work is to learn to let a young person go; to let her make mistakes, to reject Christ if she chooses to, and to desert the fellowship. There is a strong temptation to use every means, fair or foul, to hold on. Emotional pressure from a well-intentioned adult can easily violate a young person's integrity. But if God lets people go, so must we, no matter how difficult and painful that may feel.

God stands outside time. His schedules are not always ours. We can unwisely precipitate a spiritual crisis in the life of a young person which God never intended to happen then. It may be our task just to sow. God will provide someone else to water, and perhaps someone else to reap (1 Cor. 3:6–9). He will certainly never violate a young person's freedom of choice. He is the one who does the work, and he decides when it is to be done, and through whom.

On the other hand, in our relationship with God as 'adult' children we have a different liberty. The fundamental Christian response to God is faith not works, liberty not law-keeping. It is the liberty to do right, and we act out of gratitude to the God who has done so much for us. We live under grace and by faith. Day by day we have to explore which of various grey options is right for us now.

So in youth work we have to help young Christians to cope with a world in which issues are rarely black or white. For young people, legalism is all too easy and it is often the immature Christian response. There are clear biblical principles, and we have the presence of the Spirit to guide us as free sons and daughters, but there are often no set rules to pass on. The Christian life is essentially a relationship of love. Our ultimate moral authority is a person and not a principle.

It is the youth worker's task to help young people make this transition in a culture where (almost) anything goes, and everything changes. We have to wean them away from that, without encouraging them into legalism on the one hand or a weak 'just do the loving thing' on the other. The Christian does not weigh up each situation on its merits. There are fixed biblical principles, and, above all, a clear moral authority in the person of Christ. But it is not always easy to discern his will. We will not always get it right. The mature Christian is prepared to wrestle humbly with complicated issues, trusting God's grace more than his or her own moral ability. It is only the immature who claim certainty in areas (like pacifism or baptism) where Bible-believing Christians have disagreed for centuries.

Blood is thicker than water

The pattern of fatherhood that God provides is important both for family life and for youth work. In fact, there is a considerable overlap between the two.

The cultures of the Old and New Testaments presuppose a large extended family. In our society we have single-parent families, and families where the parents have remarried, perhaps several times. We have families where the children live with mum and 'mum's boyfriend'. And we have the nuclear family of parents and a couple of kids, possibly separated by some distance from other relatives. So we find it harder and harder to understand the sense of corporate solidarity that was present in the Old Testament family. The people of Israel did not question God's justice in punishing 'the children and their children for the sin of the fathers to the third and fourth generation' (Ex. 34:7). They accepted a corporate dimension to human life which is almost completely alien to us, especially as we become more and more familiar with the fragmentation of family life.

We have already talked about the biblical balance between corporate solidarity and individual responsibility, and how it relates to the conversion of a young person. We saw there how our cultural world view makes us exaggerate the individual at the expense of the corporate. We need to correct that balance, particularly if we want to understand how the young person relates to his or her family.

Each young person is a part of their family background, however shattered that family may be. We will never fully understand the individual until we first understand that in some senses children do suffer for the sins of their parents. Without falling into the mire of determinism, we need to recognise that each person is at least partly the product of their family background.

Some young people are trapped in a cycle of deprivation and sin that distances them from Christian morality. When the church allows middle-class culture to affect and distort Christian morality, it makes the gap appear wider still. Other young people are trapped in a cycle of acquisitive materialism that distances them from Christian morality too. Others still are trapped into the 'so what?' apathy of relativism which again makes Christian morality seem about as relevant as the Jacobite rebellion to a sixteen-year-old.

Of course, family background may have quite a different effect. Abraham's offspring were to benefit from the covenant that God made with their ancestor (Gen. 17:7–8). It was an agreement made not just with an individual, but with his descendants who were considered present in the person of their forefather. The father's relationship with God benefited the children for generations to come.

There is an interesting reference in 1 Corinthians 7:14, where Paul is dealing with the possibility of divorce when one partner is a Christian and the other not: 'For the unbelieving husband has been sanctified through his wife, and the unbelieving wife has been sanctified through her believing husband. Otherwise your children would be unclean, but as it is, they are holy.' Our strong western individualism does not find it easy to make sense of such verses. For that very reason they probably have all the more to teach us. The union between husband and wife and the unions between parents and children are so strong that they must be taken into account on the spiritual level.

So Christian youth work must recognise this corporate solidarity. It does not negate the autonomy which God has granted to the individual, but it does balance it. So when dealing with a young person, the Christian worker is dealing with a family (however depleted or remote) as well. And families usually have parents: 'Youth workers and parents need each other. In most cases, the task of raising healthy, well adjusted teenagers who are growing in Christ is just too big and too complex for either parents or for youth workers to pull off alone.'[12]

The Bible does not allow us to regard our work simply as a series of case studies of individuals. In every case we are involved with the family too. In entering into a relationship with an individual we have entered into a relationship with her family. We have therefore incurred certain responsibilities towards that family.

Christian youth workers have to work out what this means in practice, but they will certainly want to visit the homes and to establish a relationship with the families of their young people. If they do not, they are failing to grasp what the Bible teaches about humanity, and the way we are organised into families.

There will, therefore, be a big difference between dealing with young people from a Christian background and those from a non-Christian background. It may not always be easy to judge accurately how Christian any particular home is, but it will always be valuable to discover whether Christian values are being affirmed or denied in a particular young person's home life.

The young person from a Christian home

If the young person's home is a Christian one, it will be a most effective means of discipling that young person. If the Christian faith is caught as much as taught, then the most powerful place for that to happen is at home. Communication goes on in the family even when no one is talking. The silence over the breakfast table, the knowing look, or the quiet things we do for one another, all communicate at a deep level. Whether we like it or not, our value system is being steadily transmitted to our children. They may neglect it or reject it, but they certainly know what it is – perhaps even better than we do ourselves!

The Old and New Testaments both take for granted that the normal context for the nurture of the young in the faith was the home and the family. We have looked at a number of Old Testament examples, and we know a little about Jesus' earthly upbringing (e.g. Lk. 2:52).

We have no examples, however, of second generation Jewish Christians in the New Testament. The nearest would be Timothy, and we know he learned from his mother and his grandmother, presumably at home (2 Tim. 1:5; 3:14–15).

The home is certain to be powerful in discipling, but faith is not hereditary. There is a well-known verse about parents in Proverbs, 'Train a child in the way he should go, and when he is old he will not turn from it' (Prov. 22:6). It is a general statement about how family relationships normally work. It is not a promise nor an inflexible law. The book of Proverbs is aimed at children as well as parents – both have their parts to play.

Moreover, that verse is not only referring to a 'way' of good behaviour. 'The training prescribed is literally "according to his (the child's) way" implying, it seems, respect for his individuality and vocation, though not for his self-will . . . the stress is on parental opportunity and duty.'[13] Parents are to help their children to develop according to their own particular bent, as God meant them to be, by affirming what each child is. But, however well they do it, they will not be able to ensure that each child believes.

Indeed, they will want to be cautious that the de-parenting process does not lead to a natural rejection of the parents' faith in the teenage years. As a young person moves out from the family, he will naturally want to question and test beliefs he had previously taken for granted. The teenager becomes aware that he does not have to grow up like his father. In his search for his own identity, he may try on other adult identities to see how he likes them. Part of that search may well entail trying out a different set of standards and values to those experienced at home.

Growing up is a good and natural experience. The exploration and testing of values and beliefs is important because it is the main way a young person appropriates them for himself. The Christian family must allow for this. It is here that parents and youth leaders can work together.

The youth leader will know that Christian values are probably being communicated more effectively at home than at the youth group. More to the point, they have been communicated for many years. On the other hand, the young person may be badly in need of other Christian adults to relate to, so that he can try on other identities and distance himself from the family life without having to reject his parents' faith as well, in his search for his own individuality. The youth leader will therefore need to back up and support the parents, not undermining their values, while at the same time helping the young person to develop a firm and stable faith of his own.

The problem of the PK

There may be special problems where a particular family is very deeply involved in Christian service. But this has particular opportunities too, as long as the family is not sacrificed for the ministry. PKs (preacher's kids) have great opportunities for making lots of friends and for developing social skills with a wide range of people. They should be able to see a lot of their parents if they are home-based, and they should have the opportunity of learning the faith from those who understand it and are skilled in communicating it. But, sadly, it does not always work out like that.

Many of us will know the truth of Murphy's Law for 'Sunday school' teachers – 'Once a Sunday school class is set in motion, all disturbances originate with the minister's son.' In these families there can often be resentment among the children that so much of their parents' time and energy seems to go on the life of the local (or wider) community of believers. Rightly or wrongly (perhaps too often the latter), the family has had to make sacrifices for the sake of the father's, and possibly the mother's, ministry. They may feel that they never have their father to themselves, that they are always having to share him, and that they have to compete for his attention with other pastoral concerns.

It is vitally important that the children of such families build strong relations with other Christian adults. They must see the faith modelled by other grown-ups, with whom they get on well, and who are quite separate from their families.

Perhaps the fellowship owes it to such families to take special care with their children. The fellowship has benefited from the time and energy that the parents have given in ministry to other Christians. The church can now repay the children by the youth leaders giving extra attention to them.

But often the opposite is the case. Our attitude can be, 'He's just the pastor's son, so he's not a very important part of our planning for the youth group, because, after all, he's going to get it all at home anyway.' Or we may be intimidated by the fact that she's the vicar's daughter, and subconsciously steer clear, because news will get back home of what average youth leaders we are. Or we may let ourselves think that youth work which is confined to the children of church families is in some way spiritually inferior to youth work which is designed to reach outsiders. But there are no biblical grounds for thinking that.

Our priorities probably ought to be the other way round. All local church-based youth work ought to start with the children of the families who already attend the fellowship, because if we cannot nurture our own children properly in the faith, what is the point of trying to win other people's children? We must aim to make disciples, and not just converts.

On top of that, Christian parents *need* the help of other Christian adults, and perhaps especially when their children become teenagers. Vicars, pastors, ministers, and full-time Christian workers of all sorts particularly need the help of the rest of the fellowship in bringing up their teenage children. However well-ordered the Christian home, the children within it will always benefit from developing relationships with other adult Christians during adolescence. This need is increased by the nuclear family which does not contain the Christian uncles, aunts, grandparents and older cousins who might have been present in an extended family.

Special care

So the wise youth leader will think carefully about the special needs of young people from Christian homes, particularly from homes where a parent is involved in full-time Christian work. These young people may well have grown up believing, and be unable to look back to a period of their lives when they were conscious of not being Christians. Like Timothy, they may have taken in the Christian faith with their mother's milk: 'from infancy . . . have known the holy Scriptures' (2 Tim. 3:15).

A heavy stress on the need to be converted and to have a 'before' and 'after' testimony will not be helpful to them. In their case, it is not the initial step of commitment, but working out what it means to follow Jesus Christ day by day, that is important. They will need help in developing their faith to keep pace with their physical and mental development. As they discover each new power and ability, it has to be handed over to the lordship of Jesus, or they will find themselves facing adolescence equipped with a 'Sunday school' faith.

Having said that, many teenagers who have been brought up as Christians, and those who have drifted into the kingdom of God, find it helpful to be able to look back to a particular date when they 'inked in' their commitment. So some element of personal challenge will be appropriate. But make sure it is not repeated *ad nauseam*, encouraging the 'annual renewal' kind of teenage Christian who thinks that Christianity is some sort of ecclesiastical insurance policy, with the premium falling due at camp each summer.

Of course, some of those who grow up inside a strongly Christian home have not yet found a personal faith in Jesus for themselves. For them, Christianity is just an outward show with which they are over-familiar. They know only too well how to act out the part. The wise youth leader will want to bring them to their own point of personal decision, getting them to see that they cannot expect to cope with life (and death) on the strength of a second-hand faith.

Sometimes a young person from a Christian home asserts her individuality by expressing her faith in a markedly different way from the way her parents express theirs. She may choose to join a different fellowship or denomination. Her parents may find this painful and may need help in coming to terms with it. And the youth leader may be in a very good position to provide that help.

Above all, the leader will need Spirit-given discernment and humility to identify the young person's particular needs and to endeavour to meet them. It will require a sound and mature theology which does not have to see each young person jump through an identical hoop of conversion, like some performing dog at a circus, but which does have a passionate concern that they should each individually accept Christ's lordship for themselves and learn to live it out in every part of their lives.

It will be clear from what we have already said that youth leaders need to support the Christian parent. We may want to encourage the church leadership to include regular teaching on Christian parenthood for the whole church. Many parents are desperate for support and instruction in this task for which modern society (by removing the extended family) has prepared them so badly.

The youth leader will certainly want to have good lines of communication with the Christian parents of his young people. Keep them well informed of the youth group programme, so that they can pray intelligently for what is happening. If you produce a programme card, make sure the parents get a copy. We may want to enlist parents' help with transport, hospitality or funds. If we do so, we will usually find them extraordinarily well disposed towards what we are doing for their teenage children.

All the time, however, we recognise that our role is a secondary and servant one. Under God it is the Christian parents' task to nurture their children in the faith. The youth group leader's task is to assist that, never to replace it. So, encourage parents to fulfil their rightful role, offering help and, where appropriate, counsel. We must resist every temptation to look down on parents or to teach their children to do so (however much it might win applause from the young people, particularly in their negotiations with authoritative Christian parents).

On their side, wise Christian parents will give their church's youth work all the support they can. They will appreciate its importance in the life of their own children. They will look for ways to support it practically and financially, and to press its case with the adult leadership of the church. They too will resist any temptation to be disloyal to their local congregation making sure that 'roast pastor' does not become one of the regular courses at Sunday lunch!

The church as family

It may be worth noting at this point that there is a sense in which the Old Testament extended family has been superseded by the church. The Old Testament put great emphasis on religious instruction within the family. The only 'youth leader' it seems to know anything about is the parent. Jesus' teaching widened the concept of family.

> While Jesus was still talking to the crowd, his mother and brothers stood outside, wanting to speak to him. Someone told him, 'Your mother and brothers are standing outside, wanting to speak to you.'
>
> He replied to him, 'Who is my mother, and who are my brothers?' Pointing to his disciples, he said, 'Here are my mother and my brothers. For whoever does the will of my Father in heaven is my brother and sister and mother.' (Mt. 12:46–50)

Jesus introduced a new community to the world, a community inspired by loyalties stronger than those of kinship.

> 'I have come to turn "a man against his father, a daughter against her mother, a daughter-in-law against

> her mother-in-law – and a man's enemies will be members of his own household."
>
> 'Anyone who loves father or mother more than me is not worthy of me; anyone who loves his son or daughter more than me is not worthy of me; and anyone who does not take his cross and follow me is not worthy of me.' (Mt. 10:35–38)

So it is not surprising that Paul picked up the terminology of the family and applied it to the church:

> I am not writing this to shame you, but to warn you, as my dear children. Even though you have ten thousand guardians in Christ, you do not have many fathers, for in Christ Jesus I became your father through the gospel. Therefore I urge you to imitate me. For this reason I am sending to you Timothy, my son whom I love, who is faithful in the Lord. He will remind you of my way of life in Christ Jesus, which agrees with what I teach everywhere in every church. (1 Cor. 4:14–17)

In fact, fatherhood is Paul's favourite picture for his own discipling: 'For you know that we dealt with each of you as a father deals with his own children' (1 Thes. 2:11).

The mandate laid on the family by the Old Testament to pass the faith down the generations is now extended to the church. Within that wider family, some of the tasks of the parent may justifiably be transferred to other adults. So there is a special place for the teenage peer group, led by adults other than the teenagers' parents, within the life of the local church.

Clearly, however, the family was still important in the New Testament church, and so we cannot just leave it to youth leaders. Jewish Christian children would almost certainly have been taught the faith within the family. We have already referred to the case of Timothy, who was a second (or third) generation Christian – it would appear from Paul's second letter to him that he learned the faith at home from his mother and grandmother (2 Tim. 1:5; 3:14–15). But then, of course, the local church might have met in his home, so there was not the clear division we know now between what happened 'at home' and what happened 'in church'.

We do not know of any example in the New Testament or the first centuries of church history of a teenage peer group under Christian instruction, but that does not rule out youth fellowships now in our very different culture. Formal academic education has now been transferred from the home to official institutions called schools. This is a cultural development, but it may indicate that a similar development in Christian nurture is appropriate for the sake of cultural relevance.

A more telling argument for the development of youth fellowships is the way the Old Testament concept of the family is extended to the community of believers, so that some of the activities of the family are now rightly transferred to the wider family of the church.

It would be wrong, however, to use this argument to play down the importance of the home. Many of the New Testament passages we have already looked at in this chapter make it clear that the home and the family are vital, and we neglect them at our, and the young people's, peril.

The young person from a non-Christian home

There are all sorts of reasons why people today need extended families. The church's ability to provide such a family (particularly one bound together by supernatural love) is something that makes it especially relevant to our culture. The young person from a non-Christian home background is someone who will need a Christian 'family' as well.

With this sort of young person, Christian youth work has to recognise that the home (where the most powerful communication about values is likely to go on) will be pulling in a different direction from the gospel. The non-Christian home may well stand for, or at least allow, quite different standards to those of the Christian home. Perhaps these will be different standards of honesty and sexual behaviour (which are actually disobedient to God). Perhaps the non-Christian home will be involved in the good works of a man-centred 'religious' outlook. Or they may have an indifference to spiritual things, where Jesus Christ is nice enough in his way, if you want to believe in him, but also nice enough not to worry about if you prefer making money and the pursuit of personal wellbeing.

The influence of that background must always be considered while caring and praying for such young people. The youth leader can easily underestimate their ignorance of the gospel. Twenty years ago, young people in the UK would probably know something of the life history of Jesus Christ, but they would probably not understand what it meant. Ten years ago, we could not assume that young people knew even the outline of the gospel story, so we had to tell it to them before we could tell them what it meant. But now, the worldview of young people has shifted, so that they (with, perhaps, a slight exception in Northern Ireland) are oblivious to the gospel and therefore its message plays no significance in their lives. They absorb fragments of many different views of the world, and try to hold them together in an incoherent mess. Nick Pollard wrote: 'Such is the nature of today's culture that young people adopt ideas in a "Pick and mix" fashion from a wide ranging and constantly changing smorgasbord of ideas that are around.'[14]

So young people today may have no knowledge at all of the Bible, a very distorted view of the Christian faith, and a view of the world which makes them respond 'So what?' when presented with the claims of Christianity.

We have got to start at a very basic level of Christian teaching, taking nothing for granted. But before we do that, we may have to clarify for them what their view of the world is, and where it is heading. Then we will need to dismantle it gently, and to build up a Christian view instead. Both in evangelism and in discipling, a foundation must be laid of the simplest spiritual truths – 'of repentance from acts that lead to death, and of faith in God' (Heb. 6:1). It is possible for a young person to build the superstructure of an apparently genuine conversion and an apparently healthy Christian life without actually having laid the only foundation on which they can safely be grounded.

David Day and Philip May noted: 'The general lack of knowledge concerning the Bible and naiveté about the way to understand it suggested that it was seldom read and largely devalued by young Christians. In fact, the opposite was true. A surprisingly substantial number claimed to read the Bible regularly.'[15] That is disturbing, because if young Christians claim to be reading the Bible, but have very little idea about how to read it or what it contains, it points to a great and urgent need to educate them about the contents of the Bible, and about how to read it for themselves. And this situation is more probable in the case of a young person from a non-Christian background.

There may be great pain in that background too. It may be the pain of one or more divorces, the pain of abuse or sexually transmitted diseases. Of course, all these things can be present in a Christian family, but there will always be the additional pain of spoken or unspoken opposition to the gospel and antagonism to God.

The teenage years can be a problem in a well-ordered Christian family. Even there the 'negotiations' involved in the de-parenting process can escalate into ethnic cleansing at the breakfast table. But that process is further complicated in the non-Christian home when the young person is considering or has adopted a set of spiritual values opposed to those of the rest of the family. Here the youth leader will need wisdom and tact.

In these situations a youth leader may find herself in the role of the parent. Job interceded with God continually for his sons in case they had sinned in their hearts (Job 1:5). Where the parents of a young person cannot pray for her and are indifferent to her spiritual welfare, the youth leader will have to take that burden on herself.

And a Christian teenager in a family may be a significant factor in God's plans for that family – it may be God's purpose to bring the whole family to himself starting with the younger generation – but, if the family do not respond, the youth leader must continue to work within a firmly biblical frame of reference.

In other words, the fact that the young person is a Christian but the parents are not, does not overthrow the biblical order for the family. Children are not instructed to obey their parents only if their parents are

Christians. While children, they are to obey Christian or non-Christian parents. Once adult, they are to respect and honour Christian or non-Christian parents.

We must not underestimate the difficulty that young people will face if they try to share their faith with their parents. There are some remarkable success stories of children witnessing to their non-Christian parents. The gospel for the non-Christian parents of a Christian young person is largely that young person's obedience to them. If after his conversion the main difference his parents notice is that he never stops trying to evangelise them (implying in the process that what they brought him up to believe was not good enough for him), he may only end up alienating them. It is the youth worker's task to teach young people to obey their parents, before they start trying to evangelise them. If the parents notice a new and striking obedience in their child, then they are faced with a powerful testimony to the gospel which they will find it hard to ignore. A tidy bedroom is probably as good and as challenging a gospel message as some young people can communicate to their parents!

So youth workers themselves will have to model respect for parents – not only for their own parents, but also for their young people's parents. They will want to respect the parents' wishes, even when those wishes are to curtail a young person's Christian activities.

For example, when a father says that he does not want his daughter to attend the youth group again until after her exams, the youth leader should show respect for that prohibition. The youth leader might visit the father and ask him to permit a limited attendance – perhaps on one day of the week with a promise that she will personally drive his daughter home straight afterwards

– but, if the father remains adamant, the youth leader must come to terms with the fact that she is not the parent. That father will one day answer to God for the way he brought up his children, but it is unlikely that the long-term spiritual welfare of the daughter will be assisted by the youth leader encouraging direct disobedience to her parents.

Of course, there are situations where parents completely misuse their God-given authority. If a young person is forbidden to read the Bible or pray at home, then perhaps a different ethic will prevail, but such situations are rare.

Usually parents are motivated by a genuine (if sometimes misguided) concern for their child's welfare. The mature youth leader will accept that and seek to work with it rather than against it. She will always remember that the work of converting and nurturing the child is God's from beginning to end. It is God who has given us the command to obey our parents while we are children, and to respect them once we are adults. We can trust him to have got it right. The more we trust the Bible, and seek to base our youth ministry on it, the more God will be able to use us for his glory.

So there are dangers in the youth leader seeing herself as a substitute parent (although that may actually be true in some ways). Certainly we must take the home background of every young person seriously and be sensitive to the differences between a Christian family and a non-Christian family. We remember how Paul became 'all things to all men', so that he might by all means save some (1 Cor. 9:22). He adapted himself to the Jew, who would have had a stomach full of religious instruction at home, and to the Gentile, who might well have had none (see 1 Cor. 9:19–23).

Meanwhile, back in the classroom . . .

One area where adolescents spend a large part of their lives and where Christian youth work can be done is the school. Many Christian schools workers claim that the local school presents unrivalled opportunities of reaching out to young people.

All young people in the UK today have to attend school up to the age of sixteen, but, because school is seen as essentially part of the world of childhood, it is not an experience that is highly valued by young people in their aspiration for adulthood.

For some, school is a painful experience. Those in the lower academic bands often have to face a continuous set of implicit or explicit messages that they lack competence. Many will later regret that they did not do better at school, particularly as they search for employment. But all will look on their school days as part of the world of childhood and adolescence.

It will also be a place where young people experience the peer group in its most intense form. The pressure to conform can be enormous, and for the Christian teenager this pressure usually acts in a negative direction, against their Christian faith. The one who dares to be different invites scorn and isolation at a stage in his development when he is most vulnerable to what his peers think of him. It is the age when they tend to take messages about themselves more seriously from their peers than from adults. 'A teen will compromise his own identity in order to be accepted by his peers.'[16]

It is at school and college that the young Christian may find it hardest of all to live out his faith because of the overwhelming pressure to conform and his own fears of rejection by his peer group. There are two immediate lessons to be drawn here for youth work.

How's your education?

The first is that it will not be helpful to model the teaching programme of the youth fellowship on the classroom.

While it might appeal to the academically more able (the sort of person who is constantly affirmed by his academic success at school and who is bound for a university degree), it will alienate those of lower academic ability. More importantly, it will assert a cultural value, the value of academic achievement for its own sake, which God himself denies (1 Cor. 1:25–31). It will also tend to make Christianity look like part of the world of childhood, which young people want to leave behind.

Instead, it is important to teach the true value and purpose of education in the youth fellowship. Young people need to get their experience of academic education into a Christian perspective. The clever need to be taught not to despise the less clever. The assumption that education is just a means to an end (a better career or a larger wage packet) needs to be challenged. The whole notion of competition and self-improvement needs to be thought through with the help of the Holy Spirit. The Beatitudes (Mt. 5:3–8) call into question the basis of so many of our assumptions in this area.

It may be helpful to remind members of the youth group who are facing a continuous set of implicit messages at school regarding their incompetence, that many others have struggled with their school work. Einstein was apparently told by one of his school teachers that he would never amount to anything. Charles Darwin did so badly at school that his father told him 'You will be a disgrace to yourself and all your family.' The writer G.K. Chesterton was such a bad pupil that one of his teachers told him, 'If only we could open your head we should not find any brain but only a lump of white fat.' School studies are a very limited measure of human ability.

Where moral, ethical, and religious matters are being taught and debated at school, the youth leader would do well to teach the young person to defend his or her Christian faith effectively in the classroom without arrogance or ill-manners.

It is also important that the whole ethos of the youth group is adult rather than childish and school-like. It must have a serious educational thrust to it, and it must be lively, but it must also be clear that what we are communicating is essential for adult life and is not just games, even academic ones. It is a call to maturity, and the atmosphere of the fellowship will benefit from reflecting that.

Spiritual isolation

The second lesson for youth ministry is that the young Christian who is spiritually isolated at school is very vulnerable.

James Dobson reports an interesting study in *Preparing for Adolescence*: When nine members of a group of ten teenagers were instructed to vote for an obviously wrong answer, the tenth young person (who did not know the other nine had been instructed to vote wrongly) would almost always, after some hesitation, vote with the crowd against the clear evidence of his own eyes. However obvious the answer, if the nine voted wrongly, in 75 per cent of the cases tested the tenth would vote along with them, rather than stand out against the crowd.

However, it was also discovered that if just one other teenage voted correctly, then the chances were greatly increased that number ten would also do what he thought was right. If just one other person will stand out against the group, then a young person gains courage to resist the pressure to conform.[17]

In all too many schools there are young Christians walking around who never get to identify one another. They feel alone and isolated. They may never know that there was actually someone else in their class or year group who shared their convictions and was trying, like them, to march to the beat of a different drum.

Peer pressure can have a very damaging effect on a young person's faith, because for the young Christian at school it usually acts in a negative direction. But peer pressure can also be beneficial. It is a matter of exposure to the right peer group. The pressure to conform to non-Christian standards can be counteracted by exposure to a Christian peer group. This peer group does not have to be huge – just one or two others can be sufficient to be a great help in strengthening and encouraging each other to handle these pressures. Parents and youth leaders need to think positively about peer pressure and look for ways to use it on the side of the gospel, because of all the ties that hold young people to their faith, humanly speaking, the strongest by far is the association with other young people.

Young Christians need other young Christians so that they can support each other in their discipleship.

The Christian Union

This is a strong argument for school and college Christian Unions. They provide a forum where Christian students can recognise one another. They show them that they are not alone, and they help the Christian teenagers live out their faith. Of course, the evangelistic *raison d'être* of a Christian Union is most important, but here we want to concentrate on the value of the Christian Union in the encouragement and survival of the Christian teenager.

This function is sometimes called 'fellowship', but it is really 'identification' and the mutual encouragement that springs from that. By attending Christian Union meetings the young person identifies herself as a Christian in the eyes of other Christians, and of non-Christians. This is in itself an act of witness to the school or college, and it is a gesture of solidarity with the faith of the other Christian Union members. Regular attendance at Christian Union meetings by an individual Christian can by itself make a powerful contribution to the spiritual lives of the other members. As a young Christian teenager, Phil was encouraged to go along to his school Christian Union for this very reason.

(Where a Christian school teacher puts in an appearance at the school Christian Union, it can be a huge encouragement to Christian students. It may not always be wisest to take over the running of the CU entirely, nor even to attend all its meetings. But the act of identification with fellow Christians across the teacher/pupil divide is a powerful gospel testimony.)

'Fellowship' in the New Testament is not something that Christians have, as if you could just meet to 'have fellowship'. Fellowship is something Christians *do.* It may be prayer, it may be evangelism, it may be Christian teaching (it may even be suffering). Fellowship is one consequence of these activities. All of these are valuable Christian activities for the Christian Union, and the encouragement and identification which they provide is invaluable.

In the absence of good youth fellowships in the local churches, a Christian Union may have to have some of the functions that would normally belong to the local church, but this is never an ideal situation. As we saw in chapter five, nothing can adequately replace the local community of faith in the life of the believer, whatever that believer's age.

On the other hand, the local church youth fellowships are often a very effective launching pad for school and college Christian Unions. They can provide the back-up that helps to guide and support them. In fact, for many youth fellowships the local schools are the most natural spheres for evangelism. It is here that many of their members spend a large number of their waking hours in close contact with non-Christians. So the youth leader must equip his young people to witness in their schools. In order to assist that, they will need a living fellowship there in the shape of the Christian Union. They will also need the opportunity provided by evangelistic events focused on the schools (but probably better organised by the churches).

Local church youth workers may be allowed to participate in some lessons, either themselves or by bringing an outside team in for a specific period. Little will be achieved, however, by deceit – cloaking 'hit and run' evangelism under a veneer of RE respectability. Much however can be achieved by respecting the school authorities and co-operating with them to present Christianity to the pupils in an unemotional and straightforward way.

Christian school teachers themselves will certainly need the support and encouragement of local churches. Close communication between youth leaders and the Christian teachers in local schools will be very valuable in evangelising and discipling young people. When a school Christian Union run by a teacher does not try (or is not able) to link up with the youth groups of the local churches, both works are impoverished.

Understanding the educational system and the sort of pressures that face the young Christian at school today is certainly important in youth ministry, but it is not as important as having a biblical understanding of the family – of how family life ought to work, of the pressures faced by the teenager at home, and of the differences between the young person from a Christian home and the young person from a non-Christian home.

We need to continue to bring the Bible's teaching to bear on both these areas of a young person's life. We will find that it will guide us step by step with the authentic voice of the living God.

RESPONSE

1. Take your dog for a walk, or do whatever you need to do in order to have a good, prayerful think. How do you get on with your parents? If you are a mum or a dad, how good a parent are you? How well are you modelling these relationships to your young people?

   Assess how you are doing at the moment, and make specific commitments to God to do whatever you need to do to improve these relationships.
2. What priority does your home and family life have with regard to your youth ministry, your

career and your relationship with God? How much time are you spending on each? How much time should you be spending on each?

3. Write out a list of the young people in your group, and for each one, make a note of whether you have been to their home, and if so, whom you met, and other important parts of the conversation.

   For those that you have not been to, work out ways that you could get to meet their parents and brothers/sisters. You may like to deliver the next programme card personally, or perhaps you could ask to borrow something, and then go and collect it. Why not aim to do something like drop into each member's home in the next six months?

4. Note down the opportunities your church has of getting into your local schools for assemblies or for taking lessons. What do you do already? What contacts do you have? What else could the church do? Who in the church could do it? Make an appointment with your minister to talk this through, but before you go, think carefully about what you would like the church to do, and who you envisage would be able to do it.

   If appropriate, discuss this with your other youth leaders.

Notes

1 http://www.statistics.gov.uk/pdfdir/divorces0805.pdf – viewed on 26th July 2006

2 http://en.wikipedia.org/wiki/Single_parent – viewed on 26th July 2006

3 *Parenting Adolescents*, Kevin Huggins, CWR, 1991

4 *Parents and Teenagers,* Adrian Rogers, Victor Books, 1984
5 *Youth Ministry Nuts and Bolts,* Duffy Robbins, Youth Specialties, Zondervan, 1990
6 *Hide or Seek,* James Dobson, Hodder & Stoughton, 1982
7 Roland Martinson, *Group* magazine, January 1993
8 *Parents in Pain,* John White, IVP, 1979
9 *Hide or Seek,* James Dobson, Hodder & Stoughton, 1984
10 Ibid.
11 *Understanding Adolescence,* Roger Hurding, Hodder & Stoughton, 1989
12 *Youth Ministry Nuts and Bolts,* Duffy Robbins, Youth Specialties, 1990
13 *Tyndale Commentary on Proverbs*, Derek Kidner, IVP, 1971
14 Nick Pollard, Solent Christian Trust, 1994
15 *Teenage Beliefs,* David Day and Philip May, Lion, 1991
16 *Parents and Teenagers,* Barry St. Clair, Victor Books, 1984
17 *Preparing for Adolescence,* James Dobson, Kingsway, 1982

7. Hope for the Future?

Strategies for church leaders

'It will only take a couple of hours on a Friday night,' says the minister after the morning service, as he tries to persuade someone to take on the youth leadership. 'Eight till ten . . . and perhaps half an hour for preparation some other time in the week. Just to provide something for the young people. It's a case of helping out until we can find someone to take over permanently. There's just no one else at the moment . . .'

The prospective leader is not at all clear what he is being asked to do. He has a shrewd suspicion that the minister is lying, because he usually is when he says anything will only take 'a couple of hours'. He also has a vague suspicion that it is probably a life sentence, because he's heard the one about 'someone taking over permanently' before too. But he consoles himself with the thought that at least they have abolished the death penalty. The knockout punch came in the last line – 'there's no one else to do it' – and all the guilt that implies if he refuses to catch the ball before it falls to the ground.

So he takes on the youth group, another victim of immoral manipulation by someone who should know better. He hopes to be able to squeeze it into a few minutes of his already over-full schedule, and longs to be relieved of the burden at the earliest opportunity. This is a recipe for disaster and no one – not the young people, nor the minister, nor the rest of the church, nor the youth leader – is going to benefit from it. It may even be better not to bother at all.

We hope it will have become clear by now that Christian youth work is not something that can be done effectively by someone who is already busy with other things. It cannot be an added extra in local church life, tacked on because the church leader cannot bear the thought of his church not having any youth work. If it is worth doing at all, it is worth doing properly. If it is going to be done properly, it is going to require the right people, with the time and the energy to do it.

If a church is going to have proper youth work, other aspects of the church's ministry may have to be curtailed in order to release leaders for the youth work.

People not programmes

God equips his people with what they need to function as he means them to (Eph. 4:7–16). Both as individuals and as the church, he intends us only to tackle the tasks that we are capable of doing well for him. But sometimes we take on more tasks than he has equipped us for. This is particularly true of churches where the church leader overextends the ministry beyond the resources available.

Instead of doing a few things excellently for God, we end up doing a great many things, badly. We are unable to do any one thing really well because we are trying to do far too many things. The life of the local church can actually be impoverished rather than enriched by the sheer number of different activities in which it is engaged. If they are all done poorly because the Christians are so overstretched, little glory will come to God. 'Do less, better' is a slogan that some of us (and some of our churches) might profitably adopt. And in a society which seems to get busier by the year (which of the Christmas letters we received last year did *not* say the writers were 'incredibly busy'?), maybe our churches ought to be leading the way to a saner lifestyle where we have more time, and therefore more time for people, by doing less, but doing it better. Youth work is no exception. There will be times when it is better not to start youth work in a particular church, or even when it is right to close it down, because it is not a case of 'anything is better than nothing'.

We are not saying that no youth work should be started until the perfect youth leader appears. In fact, the notion of the ideal youth leader – young, good-looking, funny, musical, trendy, sporty, with a degree in theology and authentic street cred – is not helpful.

Youth work is about people and not about programmes or structures. God's answer to his people's problems is usually a person rather than a plan. He raises up people to do his work, but often people who are humanly speaking quite unpromising. This happened in the New Testament: 'Brothers, think of what you were when you were called. Not many of you were wise by human standards; not many were influential; not many were of noble birth' (1 Cor. 1:26).

And so it still happens today. God raises up people with a concern to serve him and to do his will as best they can, whatever human disadvantages they start with.

The quality of youth work in a local church will always be directly related to the spiritual quality of the people leading the work. However good the resources and structures, however sound the strategy, it is the youth leaders themselves who are the key.

We have already stressed (in chapter five) that the responsibility for youth work lies with the local church. It is the local church leaders who are responsible for the young people of their fellowship and of the area, just as much as they are responsible for the adults. It is they who should expect God to lead them regarding the youth work and to equip their congregation for it.

Let us see how the leadership of the local church can fulfil these responsibilities. As the key to youth work is people, it is the task of the church leadership to enable the right people to do the right job in the right way. Many church leaders complain that they just do not have anyone to be youth leaders, but it might be helpful for them to think about what they can offer a youth leader from their side.

A five-point strategy for youth work

1. Commitment and prayer

'The youth leader is not only a very influential person, but also a very vulnerable one.'[1]

The first thing a youth leader needs to receive from the church leadership is a strong sense that the church leaders are as committed to the task as she is. In appointing a youth leader, or preferably a team of youth leaders, the minister is not passing the buck for youth work. Responsibility may be delegated, but it is not abrogated. He must not wash his hands of the matter and hope he will hear no more about the young people for the foreseeable future.

The 'it's-all-over-to-you-now' attitude does not reflect the shared ministry of the New Testament. Jesus sent out the seventy-two disciples two by two (Lk. 10:1). Paul was constantly teaming up with people and seems to have been far from happy when he found himself alone (2 Tim. 4:9–18). Youth work is particularly demanding in time and energy, and it drains the emotions of those involved. Youth leaders must know that the rest of the church leadership is committed to what they are doing, is interested in how the work is developing, and is available to give support, advice and encouragement. 'To find an encourager is one of the greatest benefits of teamwork in the body of Christ.'[2]

Practically, this will entail a regular system for reporting back, and structured prayer support. If the youth leader is working in a particularly exposed situation – where there is little or no Christian nucleus to start from, where the young people come from disadvantaged backgrounds, or where he is expected to break into new territory – he will need a special support group whose task is to monitor and pray for his activities. The members of that group should be selected by the church leaders and the youth worker together. It is important that he does not feel isolated.

The ideal will be to form a team of youth leaders. It is not always possible at first, but the Bible is clear that God does not mean us to be alone in ministry. Husband and wife teams can be effective, but a team that includes the married and the unmarried will have greater wisdom, greater flexibility and a greater ability to relate to different young people. It will need to include both sexes.

To speak of a team of youth leaders (in the plural) may be hopelessly idealistic in terms of the realities of much local church life, but if the ideal is valid, the question is: how does the church leadership take one small step in that direction? The answer is: by its own commitment to, and prayer for, young people's work.

Many ministers think they will give serious attention to the needs of young people when somebody suitable to be a youth leader turns up, but if they started to pray for and be concerned about young people they might be surprised how quickly a suitable youth leader appears. And the answer to the prayer may well take the form of having our own eyes opened to the sort of person who would be a good youth leader. When Phil stopped leading one particular youth group, the vicar's appointment of his successor was a master stroke. The individual concerned was one of the least likely, but most effective youth leaders Phil had ever met. God guides his people as they walk, one step at a time. The first step is commitment and prayer. This step comes before starting any actual youth work.

2. *Vision and planning*

It is the task of the church leadership to have a vision for the whole church. It is also their task to communicate that vision to each part of the church, and to let each part of the church know how it fits into the overall vision. The Authorised Version translation of Proverbs 29:18 reads 'Where there is no vision, the people perish . . .' For the sake of the people, the church leadership must ask God to give them a clear vision of what he wants to happen in that congregation. Then they will need his help to share that vision with his people.

Paul seems to have had plans and a strategy on his missionary journeys (see Acts 19:21; Rom. 15:22–25). Like Jesus (Mk. 1:35–39; Lk. 5:15–16), his ministry was proactive rather than reactive.

In practical terms, having a vision means having a plan – or rather, planning. Planning is the first stage in turning a vision into reality. It casts a net over the future. The more energy and prayer that goes into planning, the greater the likelihood that the vision will come about.

Planning must be visionary. It must be proactive rather than reactive. Instead of looking at what is and asking how to maintain it, it should look at what ought to be and ask how to bring it about. Ted Kennedy, in his funeral oration for his brother, said, 'Some men see things as they are and say "Why?" But Bobby dreamed things that never were, and said, "Why not?"' That is the task of church leadership.

In the situation of the youth and children's work of the local church, there may be a big gap between how things are and how they ought to be. There may be nothing happening at all, in which case the church leadership must resist the temptation to let sleeping dogs lie. Or there may be a flourishing work at some age levels, but nothing at others.

A common pattern is to have fairly large children's groups on Sunday for the up-to-eleven-year-olds, and then a rapid decline (or even a complete vacuum) thereafter. The temptation here is to continue to reinforce the success of the 'Sunday school', while neglecting the youth fellowship. There may be an able 'Sunday school' co-ordinator who could be given oversight of the youth work as well. There may be someone teaching a 'Sunday school' class well, who could be moved to work with the teenagers. It may be right to inform the whole congregation of the area where the leadership believes there needs to be growth and development, and to focus their prayers on it for a year.

The youth leaders will need a vision for their work too, and this vision must relate to the vision of the church leadership for the whole church. To some extent it is the task of the church leadership to provide the youth leaders with their vision. They will always work better if they see how their work fits into the whole picture and if they feel part of a larger purpose. It will encourage them to plan for their own ministry.

If there is no planning in the rest of the church, the youth leaders will not be encouraged to plan or to have specific targets and goals for the young people. Without planning, there will be no practical expression of vision. The youth work will meander aimlessly, and then gradually subside into an existence barely worthy the name.

3. *Management*

In an unpublished survey of 103 youth workers prepared by Mark Lamport of Gordon College, twenty-seven per cent of those questioned said that they would consider leaving (or had already left) their youth ministry position because of frustrations over staff relationships.[3]

While that arises from a situation involving those employed in full-time youth ministry, the difficulties over staff relationships are often just as clear in situations where we have volunteer youth workers. And therefore we need to invest time in the effective management of our youth leaders.

In fact, the most time-consuming aspect of the church leadership's obligations to the youth work is management of the youth leaders. This consists of at least three things:

(a) A clear job description. Instead of the vague offer with which this chapter began, no one should be asked to take on a task in the local church without being provided with the clearest possible picture of what will be involved. Unless a prospective youth leader has a clear idea of what youth leadership is, he is unlikely to fulfil the role to his or anyone else's satisfaction. If the church leadership is not yet clear what is involved, then there must be proper discussion with the youth leader until both sides agree a job description.

A key element is the number of hours a week that will be involved. Few people are in a position to make an open-ended commitment of their time. Without appropriate boundaries being drawn from the outset, there will be a continual element of guilt, which will damage the leader spiritually. He will always feel that he has not done enough and that he ought to be doing more. It is the job of the church leadership to protect their people from those feelings of guilt.

The leader needs to know what he is expected to do, when he has fulfilled those obligations, and where he should draw the boundaries, so that he does not become over-committed and lose the balance of his own life. Because youth work involves opening up our lives to young people in order that they may learn the comprehensive nature of the Christian faith from us, such boundaries are particularly important.

It may be difficult to convey this picture in words alone. Where there is already youth work happening in a fellowship (or in a neighbouring fellowship), the prospective leader can first approach it as a spectator. The church leadership might suggest that he joins the present youth leaders for a period, just as an observer. Once he has had a close look at what is involved, then there can be a proper discussion about making a commitment to it.

If there is no youth work at present, and the future leader has had no previous experience, it is all the more important for him to get a close look at youth work in action. A training weekend or course is better than nothing. Going as a leader on a Christian camp or holiday for young people would be better still. Best of all, however, will be a situation as similar to his own as possible, where he can watch and reflect and discuss, before plunging in. There are many people struggling to do youth work in the local church, who have never had the opportunity to watch other people doing youth work. Where the circumstances are discouraging, with perhaps small numbers and a group that feels like stirring thick porridge, it is hard for the youth leader who has never seen anything else to have any sort of vision for what *might* be.

So the prospective leader must know what she is taking on, and there must be agreement with the church leadership about what the job requires.

(b) A contract. Despite the increase of youth workers being employed by the church it can still sound idealistic to speak of a 'contract', but proper management involves people knowing how long they are expected to shoulder a particular responsibility. Without agreement on this, guilt will raise its ugly head again. People continue in particular tasks long after they should have resigned, because they feel they will be 'letting the vicar down' if they give up.

A contract is also a convenient way of encouraging people who are not suited to youth work, but who want to stay with it, to move on to other areas of ministry. Some people stay in youth leadership long after it has become inappropriate for them. A contract can act as a useful lever to encourage them to change tack. It is not easy to justify a limited contract period directly from the Bible, but it is clear that an individual's sphere of ministry can and should change – like Moses after receiving the advice of his father-in-law (Ex. 18:13–27), and Paul after his imprisonment (Phil. 1:12–14).

There is a correct, God-given imperative that keeps us in Christian ministry: 'Woe to me if I do not preach the gospel!' (1 Cor. 9:16), but specific responsibilities within the life of the local church benefit from regular review. They do not benefit from sackloads of guilt carried by people who feel stuck because they know the church leaders will be disconcerted, discouraged, depressed or panic-stricken if they try to resign.

So it is helpful to have an informal agreement about how long a youth leader is to do the job. Just as there needs to be an induction period during which the leader can form a clear picture of the task, there also needs to be a probationary period before a firm commitment is made. The 'contract' might be for a three-month probationary period first. During that time the leader gets some first-hand experience of youth leading, and, at the end of it, he may decide that he does not want any more. Or the church leadership may decide he is not suited to it. Perhaps they can see it is damaging his marriage and his family, or some fact emerges about his past which they had not known before and which makes it unwise to have him working with young people, or the other leaders cannot work with him, or it is clear that his understanding of the job is incompatible with their expectations.

Whatever the circumstances, both the new youth leader and the church leadership know that at the end of the probation the arrangement can be ended by either party after prayerful discussion. This has several advantages. It allows the nervous leader to have a gentle introduction to youth work, without having to make a serious, long-term commitment. There are many youth leaders who would never have started at all if they had not been allowed to start gently, so that their early misgivings were gradually overcome by actual contact with young people. It also provides an extended period during which both sides can try to discern God's will accurately in the matter. It cannot be a snap decision on the spot. It has to be thought about, prayed over and discussed.

If both parties agree at the end of the three months, then the informal contract might be extended for one or two years. It is wise to keep it fairly short. The mobility of modern society increases each year and, however much the leadership may long for a degree of permanence in the organisational structures of the local church, they are unlikely to achieve it.

A short contract may actually prove a more serious commitment than a longer one. If a leader undertakes to lead the youth work for a year, after serious thought and prayer, then he is more likely to think twice when he is offered promotion in his work that entails a move across the country two months after he starts. If God led him to take on youth leadership, then God is probably not behind the new career opportunity. Christians who turn down promotion at work for the sake of their Christian ministry are a powerful testimony in our society.

Having said that, we still ought to be encouraging long-term youth work, where the youth leaders are committed to their young people throughout their teenage years. Please do not get the impression from the one or two-year contract mentioned above, that youth leaders will then have done their stint. Short contracts maintain flexibility, but church leaders also ought to be encouraging some leaders to consider real long-term commitment to their members, by keeping on renewing their short contracts. That would be the very best thing for the young people.

The idea of contracts is also good for the church leadership who are then forced to review the youth leadership regularly when the contracts terminate. 'Fire-fighting' management, which intervenes only if a crisis arises, is a poor model for Christian work. The local church needs 'hands-on' management, where the overall leadership exercises a continuous concern for the work. This need not be an interfering concern – it can be very light and trusting – but the youth leader knows that he is not forgotten. He also knows that he can step out of the work without any acrimony or guilt at a specified date.

The growing number of church-based full-time youth workers is a welcome development, but their employment by churches raises important issues regarding the way they are managed, professionally trained and accredited. This is an important area. Churches are beginning to understand and implement the responsibilities of employing someone in a full-time capacity. One particularly relevant point here is the length of contract that a church should have with a full-time youth worker. Many churches need to recognise that youth work is a profession for many, and not just a one- or two-year gap before ordination or some other career, and such matters need to be recognised in the conditions of employment of full-time youth and children's workers.

(c) Accountability. The third element in management is that the individual should know to whom she is accountable, and should expect to be assessed.

Frequent evaluation – of self and ministry – is an essential practice. Your practice of evaluation demonstrates your willingness to grow. It provides an honest look at what could be improved upon, and it offers a chance to celebrate the good things.[4]

There are biblical instances of this. For example, we see Paul reporting to the council in Jerusalem (Acts 15), and keeping in touch with his mother church at Antioch (Acts 13:1–3; 14:26–28; 15:30–35; 18:22).

Yet how many people in local church life have never been told whether they are doing their jobs well or badly? Most people soldier on, not particularly clear what their actual job is, and certainly unaware of whether they are doing it well or whether they could be doing it better. We all need assessment. Or to be less threatening, we all need to have a review from time to time. Without it we do not achieve our potential.

It is important that this is agreed upon at the beginning, however. Once someone has been doing a job in the local church for a year or two, it is very hard then to start assessing them. A new initiative to increase accountability will inevitably be interpreted as a threat – they will think that they cannot have been doing the job properly, otherwise the rules would not be being changed now. It will help, however, if reviews are introduced right across the board, and not just in the youth work.

Not only must the review be agreed from the outset, it must also consist primarily of encouragement. As many of today's young people are starved of affirmation and encouragement, so are their leaders. It is said that we need to be praised five times as often as we are criticised. Unless the review consists mainly of encouragement, any criticism offered will not be taken constructively. It will be seen as a threat, and it will be handled defensively by the recipient. But, if the main content of the review is praise, affirmation and encouragement, then we will have built a firm bridge for constructive criticism. At the same time, we must be honest – we can make people feel good about what they are doing without necessarily telling them that they are doing it well. They will be able to hear what we say without being threatened, and they will be able to improve their work in the light of what we say.

So someone must review the youth leaders – not in order to criticise them, but so that they are encouraged, so that they feel a part of the whole church, and so that they are able to become better youth leaders. This does not have to be the vicar or pastor himself. There may be a churchwarden or a deacon or an elder who will watch over the youth and children's work. But individual youth leaders must know from the start that they will be meeting someone briefly from time to time to chat and pray over their work with the young people.

If the arrangement is too haphazard, it will not fulfil its purpose because the leader will not have that vital sense of belonging to a team. Book in a time now for an informal chat in six month's time. If no arrangement is made, then 'fire-fighting' management takes over. The first time anyone says anything to the youth leaders about youth work is when something has gone wrong. Interference at this point is unlikely to be appreciated, however, when no one stood beside them and encouraged them when things were going well. It will probably cause bitterness and resentment.

Within a team of youth leaders the senior one can assess his colleagues, but he himself must be accountable to the church leadership. This is the link that is most likely to be missing. It should have been built in by the church leadership from the start. It is always worth having, and many of the problems of youth work in the local church are caused by its absence.

4. Training

Training is an aspect of management, but it is important enough to be considered separately.

This is the responsibility of the church leadership, as is the financing (or at least the subsidising) of it. We cannot expect youth leaders to take the initiative and get themselves trained. Many do, but the church leadership should make it clear right from the start that training is necessary, that they want it to happen, and that they will facilitate it. The church leadership is not required to provide the training, because it may not be able to, but it is the responsibility of the church leadership to see that it happens.

All too often people get their first training after they have been doing a task in the local church for some time, and they probably have to pay for it themselves. 'Many youth leaders would never dare even to suggest that their local church finance their attendance at a conference of particular interest and yet for the church to do just this would be a forward looking investment.'[5]

Some churches and fellowships may not be in a position to fund the training of their leaders, but most can at least subsidise it, and many can pay in full, particularly where there is a fund for the youth and children's work. Many youth leaders are prepared to pay for their own training (and are better informed on where to look for it). But this should not deter the church leadership from taking the initiative in instigating training, and ensuring that it happens.

Ideally some training should be 'on the job' and from within the local team. The principle of accountability will encourage this. The most effective training takes place when an inexperienced leader works alongside an experienced leader, when they watch each other in action and reflect together on what they are doing and how they might do it better. That is a major reason why going on a Christian camp or holiday venture is such a good idea for a youth leader, because this sort of training can be going on all the time during the event.

However, it is also helpful to go on a course or to attend a residential training conference. The church leadership should encourage the leaders to find a suitable one and, if possible, should offer to pay for it and for any travel expenses. An offer to subsidise the cost may be sufficient encouragement (if the fellowship really is unable to fund it fully).

Training is part of the initiation for youth leadership. It should not be necessary to say that it must come at the beginning rather than at the end! This is particularly important where youth work is being started for the first time, and so there is no possibility of on-the-job training. To start up local church youth work without any experience and without the prospect of any training is a hard task indeed. It would be better for the prospective youth leader to join the leadership team of another church's youth work for a time (even if it means a regular drive of some distance and a delay in starting the new youth work), or waiting to attend a suitable course or training conference first.

God equips us for ministry as we serve him. The leadership of the local congregation can expect to see that happen as their youth leaders improve with training and experience. They should build that expectation into their church life and plan to be the Holy Spirit's instrument in constantly raising the standard of the youth leaders.

One further point: we are never 'trained', so be immediately suspicious of those who think they are! Training is an ongoing and never-finished process. The best leaders are always keen to learn, and therefore keen to receive more training.

5. *Resources*

The final thing a youth leader can expect to receive from her church leadership is the resources necessary to do the work. As God, in calling us to his service, assures that he will supply all we need to serve and obey him (Phil. 4:19), so the youth worker needs to know how her needs will be met.

There may be situations where she has to be told that there are no funds available for youth work, and any money she wants to spend she will have to raise herself. That will be sad, but at least she must be told it clearly, so that she knows where she stands.

Effective youth work costs money. Money will be needed for equipment, teaching materials, subscriptions and affiliation fees to national organisations, leaders' training and books like this one! But most significantly, money will be needed to subsidise activities for the young people.

Without money for this, the activity programme will favour those members who have the money to pay for trips, outings, camps and holiday ventures, and it will exclude those who do not. The alternative is for the youth leaders to curtail the activity programme until it is within the reach of all the members' pockets, but it is far better to have the resources available to do ambitious things without favouring the wealthy and excluding the poor. If the church will not subsidise the young people's activities, then the youth leaders should set up a fund to even out the differences between the young people's backgrounds. Perhaps the youth leaders could divert some of their normal giving into this fund. This is a practical way of making sure the youth work has no bias towards the privileged.

Hopefully, most churches will budget to pay for their youth work. The church's annual budget can be a valuable planning instrument. It can be one way that the church leaders expresses their vision for the future of the congregation, and one way they put their priorities into practice. In fact, the first practical step towards starting a youth work in a church might be for the church leadership to put a figure into the budget for youth work, even though no youth work exists as yet.

Some church leaderships generously offer to underwrite the youth and children's work of the church. 'Just tell us what you spend', they say to the youth leaders, 'and we'll give you a cheque.' That may appear to be generous, but it is not the best way of operating, and it can conceal a low level of commitment to the youth work by the rest of the church. By budgeting specifically, the church can give the youth work the priority they think it should have in the church's spending. They will also be encouraging the youth leaders to plan how best to use the resources available. They may even want to suggest how the youth leaders spend the money: so much on training, so much on subsidising youth activities, etc. They will certainly want a report on how it has been spent at the end of the year.

Other churches refuse to accept any financial responsibility for youth work. Such fellowships are rare (and their leaders are unlikely to be reading this book!), but where a youth leader encounters this situation, there are still plans he can implement. The most common is fund-raising events by the young people themselves, where the money raised is divided between a charity and funding the youth work.

Some youth leaders redirect a portion of their own giving that would go to their home church specifically into the youth work, until the church takes responsibility for that work itself. It is best to do this with the full knowledge of the church leadership and the church treasurer. In fact, it is useful to ask the treasurer to administer a separate youth fund, so that the whole fellowship can know exactly what is going on and other members (particularly the parents of the young people) can contribute to the fund as well, if they want to.

It is surprising how much money can be released for youth work in this way. When Christians allocate part of their giving to some Christian work in which they are directly involved themselves, they often find themselves giving more generously than they normally would. It is also surprising how quickly the church leadership may prefer to budget properly for the youth work in the future. It will prove a wise investment.

Great ideals, but grim realities

As you have read this five-point strategy, you may have felt that it is written for a situation a million miles away from where your local church is at the moment. We are sorry if it has sounded hopelessly idealistic, but we do need an idea of how things should work, even if that ideal is a long way away at present. We also need to be clear about the first steps we can take towards that distant ideal. 'The journey of a thousand miles begins with a single step.'

So many church leaders lament that their church cannot do youth work because they have no one to do it, but they overlook what they could already be doing to express their commitment to young people, in anticipation of God providing them with suitable youth leadership. To pray for youth work and to budget for it are the first steps to realising their vision. Until they take them, God may not do his part in answering their prayer for leaders.

This five-point strategy applies to every sort of Christian youth work. Whether the model in the church leadership's mind is of a 'closed' nurture group, or of work with unchurched kids, their responsibilities towards it are the same. If they do not fulfil them, they will be weakening the youth work and increasing the probability of it being a problem area in the church's life.

We have already argued that the distinction between 'open' and 'closed' youth work is unhelpful and theologically uncertain (see chapters three, four and five). There are biblical patterns for communicating the faith (whether in evangelism or in nurture) that should be normative for every area of the local church's life, but starting youth work in the local church may mean choosing an appropriate point on the open/closed spectrum at which to begin.

There may already be a group of spiritually hungry young people at hand, or there may be no evidence of spiritual hunger whatsoever among young people in the area. In the light of their particular circumstances, each fellowship has to create its own custom-built structure for youth ministry. In every case, however, the fellowship will be trying to discover what God is already doing and to relate their plans to his purposes. They must take seriously the Bible's guidance on how youth work should be done, and they must check their church's practices against the scriptural principles we have tried to outline in this book.

There are certain recurrent problem areas in Christian youth work. So far in this chapter we have spent some time looking at an ideal 'model' of youth work. Now it is time to get our feet firmly back on the ground by considering some of the most common problems in youth work today.

1. *The life of the leader*

Some youth work problems relate directly to the personal life of the leader. We suggested in chapter six that God has set an order of priority in every individual's relationships.

First, the church leadership must be satisfied that the youth leader has established and is maintaining his own relationship with God. Congregations are often careful to check that the youth leader is converted, but they may not be watching so carefully to see whether he is continuing to grow spiritually. His leadership of the young people must not be allowed to damage his own spiritual life and growth. This is not always easy to discern, but wise church leaders will have it in their thoughts and prayers. For example, is their church life structured in such a way that the youth and children's leaders rarely get to hear a sermon?

Second, the youth leader's relationship with his own family must not be torpedoed by the youth work. After marriage, the Israelite was excused military service for a year:

> 'If a man has recently married, he must not be sent to war or have any other duty laid on him. For one year he is to be free to stay at home and bring happiness to the wife he has married.' (Deut. 24:5)

The very recently married should take time off youth leadership. The first few months of marriage are so vital for laying the foundations of a life-long relationship that they must not be interfered with by the intrusion of young people into the emotional life of the couple (and no one can do Christian youth work without young people intruding into his or her emotional life).

It is better to delay the start of youth work for twelve months and allow the couple to lay the basis for a life-long Christian marriage. However keen they may be to get back into 'shared ministry', the wise church leader will point the eager young couple back to God's priorities. He will not put the needs of the church before their need to build a stable marriage. (The wise leader of Christian camps and holidays will exercise the same self-restraint and tell members of his team to take a year off when they get married.)

Christian youth work needs leaders who model a stable and God-centred marriage to young people. It is hard for young people from broken homes to grow up to build stable families for themselves unless they have been able to see a secure marriage at close quarters. For this reason, youth ministry may not be the right area of Christian service for a divorced person, and church leaders may want to think hard before asking a divorced person to take on this particular task. There are many other areas of the fellowship's life where that person might be better able to use his or her gifts and abilities. It is the responsibility of church leaders to try to ensure that their young people have a godly model of Christian marriage presented to them.

The third level of relationships where trouble can easily arise is when the youth leader's loyalty to the youth group exceeds her loyalty to the church leadership. Loyalty breeds loyalty, and the youth leader must know that the church leaders will not criticise her behind her back. So, for example, the youth leader must know that the youth work will not be reviewed by the church's governing body in her absence.

The church leadership cannot guarantee the loyalty of the youth leader, but they can go a long way to encourage it – by their loyalty to him, by their obvious commitment to the work he is doing, and by making it clear from the start that they will expect him to be loyal to them. If he presents the young people with a model of disloyalty to the rest of the church, he is doing great spiritual damage. And the infection could easily spread from the young people to the rest of the church.

2. *Adult church versus youth group: the great divide*

This leads to another common trouble spot in local church youth work – the problem of a youth work that is not integrated into the life of the adult church, and, in some cases, appears to have no relationship to it at all. According to comments and feedback from training events, this is the most pressing problem encountered by leaders of church-based youth groups.

As we have already suggested, the solution to this problem lies primarily in the life of the youth leader herself. If she is a deeply committed, regularly attending member of the adult congregation, her own life will be the most powerful bridge between the young people and the adult church. And like all good bridges, this one needs to be well secured at both ends. Her love for the young people and her love for the church will inevitably fuse and communicate both ways. As the young people respect and love her, they will catch her love for the church.

So, if the church leadership finds that there is a great chasm opening between the young people and the rest of the church, their first communication must be with the youth leaders. They may need to go further back in their relationship with them and make sure that they are providing them with all the things the leaders can reasonably expect of the church leadership (as listed in the five-point strategy above).

If the church leaders are being fully supportive, then they should be in a position to discuss with the youth leaders what can be done to bridge the chasm. First of all there must be good biblical teaching about the nature of the church and what it means to belong to it (see chapter five). This needs to be covered both in the church services and in the youth group.

There must also be a balance between all-age activities in the church and peer-group activities. It might be necessary to prune the youth group programme to allow the young people time and energy to participate in the life of the rest of the church. It might be necessary to make the older church activities and the main services more attractive to the young. But occasional 'youth services' by themselves rarely achieve anything. Instead, work hard to develop relationships between the young people and the older members of the congregation, and work hard to create normal Sunday services which are increasingly attractive to the young people as well as the older Christians.

There are various ways in which personal contact can be increased between the old and the young, but this rarely works at the group level. You may be able to get the youth group en masse to attend a service which they do not normally come to, but they will probably stick together as a group. The rest of the congregation may even find their group presence rather threatening. Similarly, there may be a value in getting them to lead a service in the church, but it does not usually achieve the purpose of getting the old and the young to meet one another. In fact, it can encourage the adults to regard the young people as liturgical sea-lions, brought out of their pool every so often to perform for the adults in a youth service!

It is much better to work on an individual level. Individual adults can, and should, be systematically involved in the youth group programme – as speakers, guest celebrities to be interviewed, hosts for particular activities, helpers with transport, etc. Some churches run adoptive schemes where members of the youth group are adopted by older members of the congregation for prayer and hospitality; or some of the older members of the congregation are adopted by members of the youth group for visiting and practical help. Individual members of the youth group can be invited to help conduct the ordinary services of the church. If this is done regularly and systematically, it may prove more helpful than occasional youth services, which often only serve to underline the gap between the old and the young.

The way the young meet the old most effectively is when one young person and one old person get to know and love each other. Every avenue must be explored to enable that to happen. It will happen at the level of individuals. Rarely does it happen at the level of groups.

Above all, there must be a commitment on both sides – by the adult leadership and by the youth leadership

– to the unity of the body of Christ. The Bible does not encourage us to think that we will ever finally resolve the tensions between the old and the young in this present age. These tensions will continue to exist in the life of the church, but there should be a continuous and powerful resolve on the part of the leadership (and that includes the youth leadership), not to allow them to damage the spiritual life of the congregation. It is this mutual, biblical commitment which is the fundamental solution to the problem, whatever particular strategies different church situations may require.

3. *The very small group*

A third problem area is the question of very low numbers. The study of group dynamics suggests that once a group reaches a certain size, it will build up its own momentum and be attractive to outsiders. Crowds attract crowds. But below a certain number, the group will have a tendency to lose members and to dwindle away.

This may be a valid observation of how groups usually work, and some of the findings of group dynamics may be reflections of New Testament ideas, but there are no biblical grounds for valuing a large youth group above a small one. Much current youth work thinking is moving away from the 'big is beautiful' idea, to concentrate on building relationships with a small number of young people. That is not to say that big is ugly, but maybe it is not as good-looking as some thought it was. 'Relationships are the key to effective youth ministry.'[6]

Church leaders need to guard their youth leaders against unhelpful pressure to get results in their youth work – whatever it is that we mean by 'results'. It may be the pressure of the expectations of the rest of the congregation, or it may be the pressure of a results-orientated (rather than obedience-orientated) theology. There is a right and helpful pressure that comes from a vision of God's desire to reach young people. It is his purpose that the gospel should multiply throughout the world. It is right to have ambitious goals when they are given by him, because he will then also supply the energy to reach them (Col. 1:29).

There are, however, also pressures that merely induce guilt in the youth leader. No youth leader ever did his work better while carrying a rucksack full of unnecessary guilt around with him. There are situations, particularly in rural areas, where the scope for youth work to grow is strictly limited (we know of one rural youth group where on occasion every young person in the village will be present at the youth group teaching meeting). There are other situations where the youth work may have to get smaller (sometimes drastically so) before it can grow again. Phil took over the leadership of one youth group, and started to teach the Bible, and to disciple the young people. Numbers dropped, and what was an outwardly 'successful' group began to shrivel. In time the group grew bigger again, the young people went on strongly after they left, and a lot of them got involved in Christian ministry. But when you change things and the young people start to drift away, you have to have the courage of your convictions.

Often in the life of a youth group there are growth spurts followed by periods of consolidation, when numbers may even fall slightly. Growth in the life of a youth group is not always numerical – there may be relational growth between the members, or growth in their knowledge of biblical truth, or growth in their desire to serve God in the world (although these will usually lead to numerical growth, where the opportunity for it exists). So numerical growth is not always a good and reliable sign that God is at work, but it may well be some indication, when taken with other indicators of spiritual activity.

The youth leader must know that the church leadership's support for him does not depend on his producing certain results in the youth work. He must be freed from that sort of pressure.

On the other hand, the church leadership can use the insights of group dynamics to try to create the circumstances that are most favourable to growth. Where a small group of Christian young people have a sense of isolation, it will be encouraging to link them up with other Christian teenagers. This may have to be in the form of occasional events like ventures, camps, roadshows or national events.

It may be possible to arrange some more permanent co-operation between local churches in order to create a group of young people where several youth groups come together and encourage one another. In isolated situations, money is never wasted when it is spent on transport to bring young Christians into contact with one another.

Theoretically, it is possible for several churches that have no youth work to pool their resources in order to get some started. In practice, once the youth group begins to develop its own life, there is a natural tendency for all the young people to want to attend the same church. Then the other churches feel that they have lost their young people to the chosen church. This would seem to be a much better situation than no youth work at all, but not all church leaders have the magnanimity to accept the loss of their few remaining teenagers to another church!

The small group need not be a problem where it is not seen as a problem by the leaders. It can actually represent an opportunity – an opportunity to disciple young people in more depth than is possible in a larger group. We need to remember again the way Jesus focused his ministry. It is sad to hear of a church which has closed its youth work because 'there were only a handful of young people left'. Thankfully the Son of God did not cancel his mission to earth when he only had twelve disciples and one of them a traitor!

4. *The boy/girl balance*

A further common problem in youth work is the fact that we frequently attract more girls than boys to the youth programme.

This may be a problem for the youth leadership rather than the church leadership, but it is usually a wider problem than just the youth work. Often there is a considerable imbalance in the sexes throughout the congregation. The problem may have its roots in the Sunday groups for the youngest children, where the model of grown-up Christianity which we present to the children is usually feminine. The absence of adult Christian males working lower down the age range may help to explain why more boys than girls drop out of the church's youth work at puberty. Church leaders should bear this in mind when they appoint leaders for the children's work.

Youth leaders are not always sensitive to some of the developmental differences between girls and boys during adolescence. Girls mature earlier and many youth group programmes are unconsciously designed to suit their needs rather than those of their male peers. The girls are better at handling discussions and have greater social skills. Simmons and Wade underline this distinction in the concluding chapter of their book:

> Girls, more than boys, tend to hold beliefs that are less materialistic and more to do with interpersonal relationships. Whether this is to do with some natural endowment or whether it is a function of the attitudes of the society in which we live is difficult to say, but whatever the cause it is one of the most consistent findings in this survey.[7]

Sitting around a room, studying the Bible and singing are not activities well suited to a fourteen-year-old boy whose voice is breaking and who is not at all at ease in mixed company. But his female contemporary may find this kind of meeting quite congenial. It may be necessary to correct this bias in the youth programme by deliberately adding certain physical activities for the boys. In secular open youth work, with its emphasis on activity, there is often an imbalance in the opposite direction, with more boys than girls. Many youth leaders keep a close eye on the sex balance in their groups, because they know how hard it is to attract boys into a group once it has become dominated by girls. For this reason some leaders work harder to attract and keep boys, in the knowledge that teenage girls will be attracted to a group which contains more boys than girls. This is another area where the church leadership needs to be aware of the problem and strongly supportive of the youth leaders, particularly if other members of the congregation are critical of the measures taken to maintain the balance.

All too often the youth work of the local church is weak and the church leaders feel guilty about it. We have not intended to increase that feeling of guilt in this chapter. We hope we have provided some ideas for practical first steps in establishing youth work. We hope we have also provided some guidelines for maintaining good communications and a warm and supportive relationship with the youth leaders – because that is the key that unlocks so many youth work problems.

RESPONSE

1. Ask your church leaders to read this chapter, and then fix up a time to talk to them about it, and the issues it raises (reviews, contracts, etc.).
2. If you are working in a team of leaders, instigate informal reviews with your other leaders. It is helpful to write some things down before the review, like:
   - achievements since the start of the responsibility.
   - plans for the coming year or six months.
   - areas where specific training is needed.
   - the best and worst parts of the job.
3. Brainstorm with your other youth leaders (or on your own), what you have learned about youth work since you started being a youth leader. Chat about (or think through) why/how you learned these things, and in what ways you are a better youth leader now than you were then. Pray together about what you have talked about.
4. Do you have a budget for your youth work? If not, think yourself into an ideal world, and work out what you would like to have money

for. If you have other leaders, discuss this with them, and consider making a proposal to the church leadership. How about having a specific youth fund, into which the youth leaders can direct some of their giving?

Notes

1 *The Christian Youth Manual,* Steve Chalke, Kingsway, 1992
2 *Feeding your Forgotten Soul,* Paul Borthwick, Youth Specialties, 1990
3 *Youth Ministry Nuts and Bolts,* Duffy Robbins, Youth Specialties, 1990
4 *Involving Youth in Youth Ministry,* Thom and Joani Schultz, Group Books, 1987
5 *The Christian Youth Manual,* Steve Chalke, Kingsway, 1992
6 *The Youth Builder,* Jim Burns, Harvest House, 1988.
7 *I like to say what I think,* Cyril Simmons and Winnie Wade, Kogan Page Ltd., 1984

8. Getting Down to It

A last word for youth leaders

In writing this book, our aim has been to produce a theoretical and biblical treatment of youth work as a theological foundation for the youth ministry of the local church. However, we are aware that there are many who are crying out for practical help, and they may find this through one of the resource agencies listed on pages 232–38. Inevitably that list will date quickly; addresses change and new organisations appear. It is also a personal list. We have not attempted a comprehensive survey. We are only providing the names of organisations with which we have some experience.

Not all of them would approach youth work along the lines we have suggested in this book. You can decide for yourself how true their approach is to the Bible and how appropriate their resources are for your particular situation.

You will also find a list of recommended further reading. This includes some material which we hope you will find helpful in your youth group teaching programme. But always examine published resources very carefully. Phil has been involved in writing a lot of resources. The ideas worked well with his group. But his group is not yours. So however good these published resources appear to be, they are always improved when you adapt them for your own local situation. God has appointed you to feed those particular sheep. In making us under-shepherds, God also equips us for the task. He will provide us with the judgment to know what is right for our young people and the ability to adapt material to meet their needs. We can be confident that no one knows better than we do about what our sheep need.

So have the confidence to leave things out, abbreviate sections, insert material from other sources, and provide your own explanations and illustrations. Don't leave your critical faculties on one side just because some course material comes from a well-known Christian organisation.

Some resources provided for local church youth work are excellent in terms of communication. They are right on the young people's wavelength, with good educational techniques, and a lively, humorous, attention-grabbing approach. But what they actually communicate may not be biblical at all. It may have only very tenuous links with Christian doctrine, if any. Other resources have excellent content but terrible presentation. And you have to work overtime to bring it to life and to relate it to the real world of your young people.

The danger is that the first of these two types of material is the easier to use. Your young people will enjoy it and your preparation will be easy. But if it does not teach the truths that save and sanctify men and women, then it will have no eternal value. It is going to cost us time and mental energy to prepare edible spiritual food for our young people, but it is a responsibility we must not shirk.

This book has indicated a biblical framework for youth ministry, and has sought to provide help in assessing the value of the books and agencies listed. But there are many aspects of the work that we have not been able to cover.

Youth work touches on every aspect of Christian teaching and every area of church life. Much of what we have written applies with equal force to the adult life of the church. Certainly the biblical principles of working with young people are the same as those for working with older people – we just need to apply them in slightly (or significantly) different ways, depending on whom we are working with. The strategies for church leadership in chapter seven, for example, are equally applicable to any leadership tasks within a fellowship.

The bare bones

We would like to have provided an outline of the main Christian doctrines that have particular relevance in youth work, but all Christian teaching has some bearing on youth work, and to attempt a systematic theology would be beyond our abilities and beyond your patience.

It is worth saying, however, that Christian youth leaders need to develop their understanding of certain doctrines in particular. We have already considered the centrality of the cross and the importance of a thoroughly biblical understanding of conversion.

Knowing and telling the gospel

So the youth leader must be able to explain very simply and biblically how someone can respond to the gospel. Young people are at a key stage for decision-making. They have the energy and mental flexibility and humility to consider tough issues and to change their minds about them.

There are a number of simple gospel outlines that can be learnt by heart. It would be useful for the youth worker to have one at her fingertips. Opportunities to explain how to become a Christian simply and briefly are too important to miss. Although Mark had been involved in the outward trappings of religion for twenty years, it was not until someone explained to him three simple steps to take that he became a Christian.

He told me first that I had to *admit* I was not a Christian already and that my sin had cut me off from God. He showed me Romans 3:23: 'All have sinned and fall short of the glory of God' and I saw the universal extent of sin. Then he showed me Romans 6:23: '. . . the wages of sin is death,' and I saw the inescapable consequence of my sin: separation from God and eternal death. In my heart of hearts I already knew that I did not have a real relationship with God, but now I understood why I was separated from him.

Then he told me that I had to *believe* that Jesus died on the cross to take the consequence of my sin. He showed me Isaiah 53:6: 'We all, like sheep, have gone astray, each of us has turned to his own way; and the LORD has laid on him the iniquity of us all.' And he explained that it was a prophecy about Jesus Christ. For the first time I realised that God had punished Jesus Christ for my sin, and he could forgive me because someone else had died in my place. Jesus had been separated from God so that I need not be.

Third, my friend told me that I had to *come* to God and to accept his free forgiveness. He showed me Revelation 3:20 and told me that they could be the words of Jesus knocking at my heart: 'Here I am! I stand at the door and knock. If anyone hears my voice and opens the door, I will come in and eat with him, and he with me.'

I realised that through his Holy Spirit Jesus could come into my life there and then, to take command of what was rightfully his.

So I did. I continue to have a great faith in that simple gospel outline:

1. **Something to Admit** – that I had sinned and was cut off from God (Rom. 3:23; 6:23).
2. **Something to Believe** – that Jesus died in my place to take the punishment for my sin (Is. 53:6).
3. **Something to Do** – come to him (Rev 3:20).

This outline has certain weaknesses. It does not emphasise man's rebellion, or the lordship of Christ. In their context, Jesus' words in Revelation 3:20 are not addressed to the unconverted individual. Nor does this outline highlight the cost of becoming a Christian. But it is very simple and very brief. It is easily remembered and can be clearly explained. The three steps can be turned into a short prayer around the familiar phrases – *Sorry* (that I am a sinner), *Thank you* (that Jesus died for me), *Please* (come into my heart).

Many youth leaders have used this outline, or one of their own, and many have taken to using *Two Ways to Live*,[1] another simple and very straightforward explanation of the gospel (which is also not without its own shortcomings, however). But whatever the method, the important thing is that we are confident about the outline.

In chapter two we wrote about the idea of a four-year conversion in youth work. The teaching programme of a youth fellowship should take that into account. As well as explaining the gospel person-to-person with his young people, a youth leader should have a Bible teaching programme that covers basic Christian ideas over an extended period. To work through the gospel of Mark, for example, on a regular basis with young people will mean that they are called to a decision about Jesus Christ. The teaching programme and personal counselling will go hand-in-hand.

Are you sure?

Another area of Christian teaching that is central to youth work is the doctrine of assurance. Young people who are converted need to have a clear answer to the questions, 'How can I be sure I am a Christian?' and, 'What happens if I sin?' They need to know that their salvation does not depend on their feelings, that it is not linked to how committed or enthusiastic they are, and that it is not arrogant for them to be certain. The answer to doubt is not greater excitement or deeper devotion, but a clearer knowledge of facts.

Teaching Christian assurance will involve teaching the authority and the inspiration of the Bible. That may be the point at which a young person's faith is most directly assaulted in the classroom.

The God who creates

The implications of the doctrine of creation are also important for young people. Coming to terms with their own physical appearance and their character and abilities, understanding their sexuality, developing a Christian attitude to work and unemployment, responding to social and environmental issues, will all depend on the extent to which they realise that this world and every human being were created by God and rightly belong to him. We will need to work these out in detail with our young people, tailoring the applications of the teaching to their particular circumstances.

We have not dealt with involving young people in service for the community, but that would be one inevitable application of Bible teaching about the creation and about worship. If God is involved with the world he made, then his people must involve themselves with it too. If he longed to gather people under his wings (Lk. 13:34), then his children must also reach out to them in love. Social involvement and evangelism should both spring out of good Bible teaching. They will both be on shaky foundations unless the young people first understand why they are doing them. We have sometimes been better at telling young people to get involved in social issues and in evangelism, than we have been at teaching them why they should do so.

Doctrine and ethics

We have touched at various points on the rampant materialism of western society. Young people will never cope with the pressures to acquire more and more possessions and to seek an ever higher standard of living unless they are clearly taught the doctrine of stewardship. When they realise that nothing we ever have belongs to us, then they will be able to get their possessions into a right perspective.

They will need to be taught the biblical basis for Christian behaviour. The emphasis must fall on the cultivation of a Christian mind, not the purchase of a quick-frozen Christian behaviour pattern. Young people need to learn *how* to think about ethical problems, more than *what* to think about them.

Although we have been referring frequently in these paragraphs to teaching doctrine, remember that the process of communicating these priceless spiritual truths is far more total than simple academic teaching on a classroom or seminar model. First, the youth leader himself must understand and live out these truths. Sometimes our greatest need in youth work is not to *teach* truth better, but to *understand* it better. Proper understanding will lead to better obedience. And then we will communicate it to our young people through our lives and our lips, even though we may feel incompetent as teachers in an academic sense.

At the same time, we need to remember that young people have a mental ability to grasp and remember new facts which they will not have when they are older. It is a good time for learning. In particular, they will never find it easier to learn verses than when they are young. Many youth leaders think that the learning of Bible verses went out with the demise of Spam as part of our staple diet, but the teenage years present a great opportunity to learn them. This should be a regular part of every youth group's life (Ps. 119:9–11).

Through all teaching in youth ministry, the gospel will be central. It is the core of youth evangelism and the core of youth discipling. It is not something we ever get beyond in the Christian life.

Counselling

Counselling is another aspect of youth work that has the gospel at its heart.

We have suggested that the most effective part of our work with young people will be where we focus our attention deeply on a few. Here we will build deep and lasting friendships which God's Spirit can use to build up both them and us. But it is not easy. We will need determination to persevere in offering friendship, even when a young person goes through an antagonistic stage and spurns that friendship. We will need restraint, so that no unfair moral pressure is put on the young person. We will need maturity so that we can accept rejection and can allow the young person freedom and dignity to choose his or her own path. We will need sensitivity to the traumas and pains of adolescence. We will need to be aware of all the emotional undercurrents which run around a teenage peer group, and which sometimes make the social times the most painful parts of the life of a youth group.

Good youth leaders watch the socio-dynamics of the youth group and try to look beneath the surface of what is happening. They try to be aware of the pain and the hurt, and to feel the pressures that their young people are feeling as they search out their own identities.

Skill in relating at this personal level can be improved when a team of leaders help one another by praying together and discussing their young people's needs. In the three youth groups that Phil has led, he has always tried to get the leaders together once a week to pray, just for thirty minutes, and usually tagged onto something else so that it does not take up yet another evening. Those brief meetings are vitally important for the young people.

The value of a regular meeting of the youth leadership team will have become obvious much earlier in this book, but one of the most useful things to do at a team meeting is to analyse the group. The leader can circulate a list of the main members of the group and ask the other leaders to write down where they think each member of the group is at the moment, what they think that member's main spiritual needs are, and how they think the group could meet those needs.

Discussing each leader's insights into the individuals in the group can be a helpful exercise for the team (even if the team is only two leaders strong). Discussing how the group programme can meet those needs may be more profitable still. It may even revolutionise what you are doing. It will certainly lead to a recognition that many of the members' needs can be met only at a personal level.

The leadership team will be able to detect the spiritual links that God is building between particular leaders and particular members. It will be able to check those relationships when they become unhelpful. With adolescents it is inadvisable for male leaders to develop a counselling relationship with girl members, or female leaders with boy members. If you are in a one-to-one situation with a young person, be somewhere where you can be seen (but not necessarily heard), tell someone 'I'm going to have a chat with Chris', and avoid forms of physical contact which can be easily misconstrued. Do all that you can to avoid putting yourself or any of your young people in a position of temptation. Be above suspicion.

A youth leadership team must always be aware of the dangers of counselling situations, especially when faced with sexual temptation. Firm or, if need be, drastic measures should be taken quickly. The advice and intervention of other leaders will be indispensable. The simple expedient of passing individual members of the group on to a leader of the same sex for counselling is a basic rule of youth work. So, for example, the sole male leader of a group made up largely of older teenage girls *must* look urgently for a female colleague.

Secular or Christian counselling courses and anything written about adolescent psychology may help us to be better at talking at a personal level with our young people. But we must develop the skill to feed the spiritual life of the ordinary young person in our group, and not assume that Christian counselling is limited to helping those with problems. It is certainly helpful to study the various counselling techniques: listening, evaluating, interpreting, probing, questioning, teaching, confronting, self-disclosing, encouraging, reflecting, and using silence (when some of the most significant, life-changing insights often come).

Whatever assistance we find to help us to do it, we must develop the ability to speak one-to-one about spiritual things. For most young people their deepest needs will not be met until someone sits down alongside them and applies Christ's teaching personally to them. Many Christians were involved in a Christian community for some time, without being converted, until someone spoke to them personally about their relationship with God. Then they came face to face with Jesus Christ and surrendered their lives to him. The first time anyone spoke to Phil about Christianity at a personal level, as an eighteen-year-old on a youth group holiday, is the time he looks back to as the moment which cemented his Christian commitment. We all have a great ability to apply what we hear to everyone else rather than to ourselves. It is only when someone says 'How about you?' that we are forced to face the truth.

Even after we have become Christians, we retain, and indeed refine, this ability to avoid personal application of our faith to our lives. Throughout our Christian lives we need those who will lovingly confront us with the truth about ourselves. The gospel is the heart of this ministry, for the unconverted and for the converted.

It may sometimes be too soon to go over a simple gospel outline (like the three steps on page 215) with someone, but it is never too late. It is not very helpful to impose a detailed explanation of how to become a Christian on a spiritually indifferent young person. Until God's Spirit starts to work on his heart, the gospel will be like a pearl to a pig (Mt. 7:6), but the converted young person never tires of hearing the gospel and needs to apply its truth to his life constantly.

The whole of the Christian life is about getting rid of sin. The unconverted person has to repent, but so does the converted person; and to keep on repenting. In the letters to the seven churches in the book of Revelation, many of the Christians addressed must have had fine records of Christian service, but those who had lost their first love were not told to pray more, or to fast, or to seek for some wonderful new experience. The Lord told them to repent. Those who were compromising were not told to pray all night for revival. They were told to repent. The lukewarm Laodiceans were not told to serve more zealously. They were told to repent (see Rev. 2 and 3). So should we, and we must teach our Christian young people to do the same. We never leave the foot of the cross in the Christian life. Those who call this emphasis pietistic, and turn young people's attention instead to the huge social and political problems of our world, condemn them to addressing that agenda out of guilt, and not out of gratitude.

Others claim that we need to get involved in the social, political, economic, moral, legal and environmental issues that face us in our society today because by doing so we are being the gospel to those we get involved with. That is a dangerous theology – dangerous because it is removing the gospel from its historical anchor in the death and resurrection of Jesus Christ.

The tasks before the church are indeed huge, and young people must tackle them, but they will only find the strength for that work when their hearts are full of thanks to God because their sins have been put away, and forgiveness is their daily experience.

Grace is the heart of Christian theology and gratitude the heart of Christian ethics. In youth work, if we remove grace from our theology, guilt rather than gratitude will become the main motivating force for Christian behaviour. Guilt saps young people's strength. Gratitude frees them for service.

Christian youth counselling must focus on telling young people the news that God loves them, that he will forgive them because Jesus died in their place, and that his Spirit wants to take control of their lives to make his kingdom an increasing reality in this present age.

And finally . . .

There have been points at which we have felt the need to try to correct some youth work practice, because it has seemed to us that it is not taking the Bible seriously. Youth work often pays lip service to the authority of the Bible, but the sufficiency of the Bible to guide and direct youth work is not acknowledged in practice – at least not very often, and not very publicly.

In trying to correct this, we may have failed to stress the excitement of working with young people. It is always exhilarating to serve Jesus Christ, but to be called to work among young people is particularly thrilling.

The furious pace of change in our society means that today's young people will grow up into a very different world. None of us knows quite what that world will be like, or quite what challenges will face the church of the future, but equipping young people for that future is one of the most worthwhile tasks in Christian ministry.

A new generation of Christians who grow up knowing the Bible and loving the Lord Jesus has huge potential. There may be a future Christian leader in our youth group, drinking our coffee, and ruining our settee, who will affect the national life of our country as much as John Wesley did.

The challenge for youth workers is to do God's work in God's way. Right practice will require right theology. The search for a correct theology will take us back to the Bible. We must read it humbly and expectantly, and we must keep reviewing our youth work in the light of what we find in its pages.

We must let it set our priorities. If we had to emphasise again any of the points we have been making, it is that the main strategic error in youth work is to ignore Christ's command to feed sheep. We concentrate too much energy on reaching outsiders through the programme and activities we offer. Spiritual impact does not come through the club premises, youth activities, events, or meetings. It comes in and through people. The most effective way outsiders are reached and drawn into the kingdom is by loving contact with those inside the kingdom. Fringe young people are drawn into Christianity by their contact with Christian young people.

So the quality of the spiritual lives of the Christian young people is the primary concern of the youth leader because they are the 'leaders' (in a biblical sense) much more than he is. Their leadership is a commitment to people, which is far more important for them than participating in decision-making, or sharing organisational control.

The organisation of youth work should not focus on programmes to present certain ideas to outsiders, but on building up young Christians to proclaim the gospel and to display the kingdom of God in practice. It is not primarily a quest for ideas that brings young people to Christ, but the quest for an authentic lifestyle. They can grasp this most easily when it is communicated through their own age group.

As Jesus lived alongside those he ministered to, and as Paul wrote 'we were delighted to share with you not only the gospel of God but our lives as well' (1 Thes. 2:8), so we must open our lives to our young people. Life-to-life communication is essential in youth work. But it will mean that we cannot minister effectively to very many people.

The main strategic error in youth work is to ignore Christ's command to feed sheep. The main tactical error is to go for quantity rather than quality. We try to influence too many people at too shallow a level, instead of being prepared to build up a few into really authentic discipleship.

One training exercise that we have used on a number of occasions when working with youth leaders from a wide range of backgrounds and involved in a wide variety of activities is this: we ask them to write down the names of the two or three young people they are influencing most deeply at this time in their ministries – the ones who in ten years' time would be significantly different because of their contact with the youth leader.

Invariably there is a pause, and each time we know that we have touched base. Some write busily, but others sit with an expression on their faces which indicates that this question has never crossed their minds before. And now that it has, they cannot answer it. They should be able to. And so should we all.

RESPONSE

1. Get a scrap of paper, blank on both sides. On one side write down the three most important things that your have learned as a result of reading this book. On the other side, write down the three things that you are going to do as a result of reading this book, and when you are going to do them. No more than three of each.
2. Pray about what you have written.
3. Go and do the things you have decided to do!

Note

1 *The Choice we all Face,* Phillip Jensen and Tony Payne, Matthias Media, 2003

Recommended Further Reading

This list is only a selection of the huge range of titles available on youth work. And it is a *personal* selection – these are books which we have found helpful in our own thinking about, and practice of, youth work. We do not always agree with what they say, but where this is the case, they have certainly stimulated our grey matter, and we hope they do yours!

Youth work theory

Express Community: Bringing Social Action to Life, Phil Bowyer, Authentic Media, 2004

Feeding Your Forgotten Soul, Paul Borthwick, Zondervan, 1993

Four Views of Youth Ministry and the Church, M. Senter (ed.) with W. Black, C. Clark, M. Nel, Youth Specialities, 2001

Growing Community: Making Groups Work with Young People, Danny Brierley, Authentic Media, 2003

No Guts, No Glory: How to Build Youthwork that Lasts, Alan Stewart, Matthias Media

Outside In, Mike Breen, Scripture Union, 1993

Reaching and Keeping Teenagers, Peter Brierley, MARC, 1993

Reaching and Keeping Tweenagers, Peter Brierley, Christian Research, 2002

The Ministry of Nurture: A Youth Workers Guide to Discipling Teenagers, Duffin Robbins, Zondervan, 1990

Youth Culture and the Gospel, Pete Ward, Zondervan, 1992

Youth Ministry, Lawrence O. Richards, Zondervan, 1990

Adolescence

The New Hide or Seek: Building Confidence in Your Child, James Dobson, Revell, 2001

Seven Ages, John Nicholson, Fontana, 1980

Teenage Beliefs, David Day and Philip May, Lion, 1991

Understanding Adolescence, Roger Hurding, Hodder & Stoughton, 1989

Understanding Teenagers, Pete Gilbert, Crossway, 1993

Parenting

Parenting Adolescents, Kevin Huggins, Nav Press, 1992

Parents in Pain, John White, IVP, 1979

Practical skills

Counselling Youth: A Comprehensive Guide for Equipping Youth Workers, Pastors, Teachers, Parents, Josh McDowell, Thomas Nelson, 1996

Do It! Active Learning in Youth Ministry, Thom and Joani Schultz, Group Books, 2000

Get Away, Arlo Reichter, British and Foreign Bible Society, 1991

Kids Taking Charge: Youth-Led Youth Ministry, Thom and Joani Schultz, Group Publishing, 1991

The Christian Youth Manual, Steve Chalke, Kingsway, 1992
Working with Teenagers, Nick Aiken, Zondervan, 1994
Worship and Youth Culture, Pete Ward, Zondervan, 1993
Young People and the Bible, Phil Moon, Zondervan, 1993
The Youth Builder, Jim Burns, Regal Books, 2002
Youth Ministry Nuts and Bolts, Duffy Robbins, Resource Publications, 2001

Programme ideas

A Different World, Phil Bowyer, Authentic Media, 2005
All Together Forever, Phil Moon, CPAS, 1992
Big Ideas for Small Groups, Patrick Angier and Nick Aiken, Harper Collins, 1992
Creative Ideas for Youth Evangelism, Nick Aiken (ed.), Zondervan, 1992
Everyone's A Winner, Jim Belben and Trevor Cooper, Bible Society, 1987
Games Without Frontiers, Pip Wilson, Marshall Pickering, 1988
Harping On?, Alan Hewerdine and Phil Moon, CPAS, 1993
Just Looking, John Allan, Bible Society, 1987
Music to Move the Soul, Steve Adams, Authentic Media, 2003
Prayer Pace-Setting, John Earwicker, Scripture Union, 1987
Prayers For Teenagers, Nick Aiken, SPCK, 2003
Pressure Points, Alan Hewerdine and Phil Moon, CPAS, 1993
Repeat Prescription, Phil Moon, CPAS, 1994
Studies 2 Go: 30 Solid Youth Bible Studies, Julie Moser, Aquila Press, 2002

Tension Getters, Mike Yaconelli and David Lynn, Bible Society, 1991
The Dramatised Bible, Michael Perry (ed.), Collins, 2004

Books for teenagers

A Sneaking Suspicion, John Dickinson, Matthias Media
Case for Christ – Youth Edition, Lee Strobel, Zondervan, 2001
God 360, Andy Flannagan, Authentic Media, 2006
Hanging in There, John Dickinson, Matthias Media
Hanging in There, Phil Moon, Monarch, 1994
Picturing Jesus, Simon Jones, The Bible Reading Fellowship, 1993
Preparing for Adolescence, James Dobson, Kingsway, 2002
Stranger Than Fiction, John Dickinson, Matthias Media
The Bible From Scratch, Simon Jenkins, Lion, 1987
The Case Against Christ, John Young, Hodder & Stoughton, 2006
The Power of Jesus, Nick Aiken, The Bible Reading Fellowship, 1993
Uncovered, Jonathan Carswell, Authentic Media, 2005

Issues

. . . and God created sex!, Chick Yuill, Monarch, 1995
Born to Shop, Mike Starkey, Monarch, 1989
Playing God: Talking About Ethics in Medicine and Technology, Tony Watkins, Authentic Media, 2006
Pure, Linda Marshall, IVP 2005
Saturated World, Joshua Harris, Multnomah Publishers, 2005
Spooked: Talking About the Supernatural, Tony Watkins, Authentic Media, 2006

Sex Is Not the Problem (Lust Is): Sexual Purity in a Lust Saturated World, Joshua Harris and Brian Smith, Multnomah Publishers, 2005

Teens Speak Out, Josh McDowell, Victor Books, 1990

The Jesus Gospel: Rediscovering the Message, Liam Goligher, Authentic Media, 2006

What Could I Be?, Peter Hick, IVP, 2005

What Could I Say?, Peter Hicks, IVP, 2000

Where is God in a Messed Up World?, Roger Carswell, IVP, 2006

Index of Resource Agencies

Probably your best resource point is the local Christian bookshop. You should be able to find there the latest youth resources and probably a video/DVD library.

We have listed below some of the Christian organisations which specialise in different areas of youth work. This is not an exhaustive list, but these are the agencies and organisations with which we have had contact.

General resource agencies

Youth for Christ (Schools, evangelism, YFC centres)
PO Box 5254, Halesowen, West Midlands, B63 3DG
Tel: 0121 5508055
Email: yfc@yfc.co.uk

Care for the Family
Garth House, Leon Avenue, Cardiff, CF15 7RG
Tel: 029 2081 0800
Email: mail@cff.org.uk

Church Pastoral Aid Society
CPAS, Athena Drive, Tachbrook Park, Warwick
CV34 6NG
Tel: 01926 458458
Email: info@cpas.org.uk

Scripture Union (England and Wales)
207–209 Queensway, Bletchley, Milton Keynes,
MK2 2EB.
Tel: 01908 856000
Email: info@scriptureunion.org.uk

Open youth work and other youth work with the unchurched

Frontier Youth Trust (England and Wales)
Unit 208b, The Big Peg, 120 Vyse Street, Birmingham.
B18 6NF
Tel: 012 1687 3505
Email: frontier@fyt.org.uk

Youth volunteer agencies

Careforce
35 Elm Road, New Malden, Surrey, KT3 3HB
Tel: 020 8942 3331
Email: enquiry@careforce.co.uk

Youth movements

Campaigners
Campaigner Ministries, 6 Eaton Court Road,
Colmworth Business Park, Eaton Socon, St. Neots,
Cambs, PE19 8ER
Tel: 01480 215622
Email: info@campaigners.org.uk

Urban Saints (formerly Crusaders)
Kestin House, 45 Crescent Road, Luton, Beds, LU2 OAH
Tel: 01582 589850
Email: email@urbansaints.org

Evangelistic agencies

Operation Mobilisation
The Quinta Christian Centre, Weston Rhym, Oswestry, Shropshire, SY1O 7LR.
Tel: 01691 773388
Email: contact@uk.om.org

Saltmine Trust
St. James House, Trinity Road, Dudley, West Midlands, DY1 1JB
Tel: 01384 454800
Email: mail@saltmine.org

Youth With a Mission
13 Highfield Oval, Ambrose Lane, Harpenden, Hertfordshire, AL5 4BX
Tel: 01582 463300
Email: info@oval.com

Student organisations

Agapé
Fairgate House, Kings Road, Tyseley, Birmingham B11 2AA.
Tel: 0121 7654404

The Navigators
Turner House, 54 The Avenue, Southampton,
SO17 1XQ
Tel: 023 80558800

Universities and Colleges Christian Fellowship (UCCF)
38 De Montfort Street, Leicester LEI 7GP
Tel: 0116 2555672
Email: email@uccf.org.uk

Aid organisations

Christian Aid
35 Lower Marsh, London, SEI 7RL Tel 0171 620 4444
Tel: 020 7620 4444
Email: info@christian-aid.org

Tearfund
100 Church Road, Teddington, Middlesex, TW11 8QE
Tel: 0845 3558355
Email: enquiry@tearfund.org

Mission organisations

A number of the missionary societies have youth secretaries and produce materials suitable for youth groups. In particular:

Crosslinks
251 Lewisham Way, London SE4 1XF
Tel: 020 8691 6111

Church Missionary Society
157 Waterloo Road, London SE1 8UU
Tel: 020 7928 8681

Overseas Missionary Fellowship
Station Approach, Borough Green, Sevenoaks, Kent, TN15 8BG
Tel: 01732 887299
Email: omf@omf.org.uk

South American Missionary Society
The Medlock Room, Handsworth Parish Centre, Handsworth Road, Sheffield, S13 9BZ
Tel: 0114 2692070
Email: med@samsgb.org

Arts Festivals

Greenbelt Festivals
All Hallows on the Wall, 83 London Wall, London, EC2M 5ND
Tel: 020 7374 2760
Email: info@greenbelt.org.uk

Bible resource agencies

Bible Society
Stonehill Green, Westlea, Swindon, SN5 7DG
Tel: 01793 418100

Scripture Union (England and Wales)
207–209 Queensway, Bletchley, Milton Keynes, MK2 2EB.
Tel: 01908 856000
Email: info@scriptureunion.org.uk

Denominational organisations

Assemblies of God
PO Box 7634, Nottingham, NG11 6ZY
Tel: 0115 921 7272
Email: info@aog.org.uk

Baptist Union of Great Britain
Baptist House, PO Box 44, 129 Broadway, Didcot, Oxon OX11 8RT
Tel: 01235 512077
Email: info@baptist.org.uk

General Synod Board of Education (Church of England)
Church House, Great Smith Street, London SW1P 3NZ
Tel: 020 7898 1000

Methodist Association of Youth Clubs
2 Chester House, Pages Lane, Muswell Hill, London N10 1PR
Tel: 0181 444 9845

United Reformed Church
86 Tavistock Place, London WC1H 9RT
Tel: 020 7916 2020
Email: urc@urc.org.uk

Youth ministry courses

Moorlands Bible College
Sopley, Christchurch, Dorset BH23 7AT
Tel: 01425 672369
Email: admissions@moorlands.ac.uk

Oxford Youth Works
Oxford Youth Works, Church Annex, Jeune Street, Oxford, OX4 1BN
Tel: 01865 204646
Email: admin@oxfordyouthworks.co.uk

Oak Hill College
Chase Side, Southgate, London, N14 4PS
Tel: 020 8449 0467
Email: clareo@oakhill.ac.uk

YMCA George Williams College
199 Freemasons Road, Canning Town, London E16 3PY
Tel: 020 7540 4900
Email: ymca.registry@ymca.ac.uk